Workshop on Multilingual Question Answering 2006

(MLQA 06)

Held at EACL 2006

Trento, Italy
4 April 2006

Editors:

Anselmo Penas **Richard Sutcliffe**

ISBN: 978-1-61738-488-2

Printed from e-media with permission by:

Curran Associates, Inc.
57 Morehouse Lane
Red Hook, NY 12571
www.proceedings.com

Some format issues inherent in the e-media version may also appear in this print version.

Printed by Curran Associates, Inc. (2010)

Association for Computational Linguistics
209 N. Eighth Street
Stroudsburg, Pennsylvania 18360

Phone: 1-570-476-8006
Fax: 1-570-476-0860

acl@aclweb.org

Preface

This volume contains the papers presented at the Workshop on Multilingual Question Answering MLQA'06, held on 4 April 2006 in conjunction with the European chapter of Association for Computational Linguistics Conference, EACL 2006.

Despite the great deal of attention that Question Answering (QA) has received in recent years due to the landmark Q&A Track at the Text REtrieval Conference (TREC), multilinguality has been outside the mainstream of QA research, which has focused mainly on the English language. Multilingual QA has emerged only in the last few years as a complementary research task, representing a promising direction for at least two reasons. First, it allows users to interact with machines in their native languages, contributing to easier, faster, and more equal information access. Second, cross-lingual capabilities enable QA systems to access information stored only in language-specific text collections.

The success of the QA track in recent evaluation campaigns at CLEF (Cross-Language Evaluation Forum) and NTCIR (Evaluation of Information Access Technologies) has shown increasing interest in both monolingual non-English QA (questions and answers in the same language) and in cross-lingual QA, where the question is posed in a source language and the answer must be found in a target collection of a different language.

The workshop intended to address a number of challenging issues for research in multilingual QA, including searching in multilingual document collections, collecting and merging answers found in documents from different languages, using heterogeneous multilingual data collections (such as the Web, XML data or data in relational databases) for answer generation, and interpreting questions in different languages. Additionally papers related to user studies or case studies where multilingual QA has played a major role were most welcome. Relevant topics for the workshop included:

- Monolingual QA systems for languages other than English;
- Cross-lingual QA systems;
- Multilingual Web-based QA;
- Case studies and user studies of Multilingual QA;
- Specific Translation techniques for Cross-lingual QA;
- The influence of translation on Cross-lingual QA;
- Multilingual QA in restricted vs. open domains;
- QA from heterogeneous multilingual data collections such as unstructured text, semi-structured data and structured data; Techniques for porting QA systems among languages;
- The effectiveness of particular techniques in different languages;
- Comparisons between QA in different languages including European and Asian languages;
- Evaluation of Multilingual QA systems;
- Resources for Multilingual QA.

The ten papers finally accepted fall in four main categories: Analysis of QA Multilingual technology, Multilingual and Translingual QA systems, QA systems in other languages than English, and finally, Adaptation of existing QA systems.

We would like to thank all the authors whose research contributions have made this workshop possible. Thanks are also due to Maarten de Rijke and Caroline Sporleder as EACL workshops chairs. Special thanks to Bernardo Magnini who promoted the idea of the workshop and to the Program Committee for their work in all the stages of the organization, from the very proposal to their careful reviewing.

Anselmo Peñas and Richard Sutcliffe

This Workshop has the partial support of the Center for the Evaluation of Language and Communication Technologies (CELCT), the Cross-Language Evaluation Forum (CLEF) and the R2D2 project (Question Answering in Digital Documents, TIC-2003-07158-C04) financed by the Science & Technology Department of Spain 2003-2006.

Workshop Organizers

Anselmo Peñas (UNED, Madrid, Spain)
Richard Sutcliffe (University of Essex[1], England)
([1]) On Sabbatical from University of Limerick

Programme Committe

Lili Aunimo (University of Helsinki, Finland)
Christelle Ayache (ELDA/ELRA, Paris, France)
Johan Bos (University of Rome "La Sapienza", Italy)
Gosse Bouma (University of Groningen, The Netherlands)
Hsin-Hsi Chen (National Taiwan University, Taiwan)
Danilo Giampiccolo (CELCT, Trento, Italy)
Brigitte Grau (LIMSI-CNRS, France)
Donna Harman (NIST, USA)
Michael Hess (University of Zürich, Switzerland)
Valentin Jijkoun (University of Amsterdam, The Netherlands)
Noriko Kando (NII, Tokyo, Japan)
Dominique Laurent (Synapse Développement, Toulouse, France)
Bernardo Magnini (ITC-irst, Trento, Italy)
André Martins (Priberam Informática, Lisbon, Portugal)
Diego Mollá (Macquarie University, Australia)
Günter Neumann (DFKI, Saarbrücken, Germany)
Carol Peters (CNR-ISTI, Pisa, Italy)
Diana Santos (Linguateca, Oslo, Norway)
Yutaka Sasaki (ATR, Kyoto, Japan)
Kiril Simov (Bulgarian Academy of Science, Sofia, Bulgaria)
Bill Teahan (University of Wales, Bangor, Wales)
José Luis Vicedo (University of Alicante, Spain)

Table of Contents

The conference, the workshop and the tutorials are sponsored by:

Center for the Evaluation of Language and Communication Technologies

Celct
c/o BIC, Via dei Solteri, 38
38100 Trento, Italy
http://www.celct.it

Xerox Research Centre Europe
6 Chemin de Maupertuis
38240 Meylan, France
http://www.xrce.xerox.com

CELI s.r.l.
Corso Moncalieri, 21
10131 Torino, Italy
http://www.celi.it

Thales
45 rue de Villiers
92526 Neuilly-sur-Seine Cedex, France
http://www.thalesgroup.com

EACL-2006 is supported by

Trentino S.p.a. and Metalsistem Group

QA better than IR ?

Dominique Laurent
Synapse Développement
33 rue Maynard
Toulouse, France
dlaurent@synapse-fr.com

Patrick Séguéla
Synapse Développement
33 rue Maynard
Toulouse, France
patrick.seguela@synapse-fr.com

Sophie Nègre
Synapse Développement
33 rue Maynard
Toulouse, France
sophie.negre@synapse-fr.com

Abstract

A Question Answering (QA) system allows the user to ask questions in natural language and to obtain one or several answers. If compared with a classical IR engine like Google, what kind of key benefits QA bring to users and how to measure their distinctive performances. This is what we shall attempt here to determine, specially in providing a comparative weak and strong points table of each system, along with showing how QA systems, in particular our Qristal QA system, requires up two to six time less "user effort".

1 Introduction

Asking questions in natural language and obtain short answers (if possible the exact answer) make QA systems the paramount of Information Retrieval.

Through TREC and CLEF international campaigns, Question Answering systems are evaluated both in monolingual and multilingual use (e.g. Voorhees, 2005; Vallin, 2005). Nevertheless, very few comparisons of performances took place between Question Answering systems and Information Retrieval engines (Kwok, 2001; Radev, 2002; Buccholz, 2002; McGowan, 2005). If so, they mainly focus on the quality of the supplied answers and on the time for user to obtain the answer.

We hereby attempt to define an evaluation method to compare performances and user-friendliness of both Question Answering systems and Information Retrieval engines. We will apply this method to our system Qristal and to the Google Desktop Search[1] engine..

[1] Google Desktop Search : http://desktop.google.com/

2 Background

2.1 Qristal pedigree

Qristal (French acronym of "Questions-Réponses Intégrant un Système de Traitement Automatique des Langues", which can be translated by "Question Answering System using NLP") is, as far as we know, the first Multilingual Question Answering System available on the consumer market (B2C). It handles French, English, Italian, Portuguese or Polish.

Qristal allows the user to query on a static corpus or on the Web. It supplies answers in one or any of the 4 languages.

Our system is described in detail in other papers (Amaral, 2004; Laurent 2004; Laurent 2005-1; Laurent 2005-2). Qristal is based on our Cordial syntactic analyzer and extensively uses all the usual constituents of the natural language processing, while, as seldom found, remarkably featuring anaphora resolution and metaphor detection.

Originally developed within the framework of the European project TRUST[2] and M-CAST[3], our system has evolved, over the last five years, from a monolingual single-user program into a multilingual multi-user system.

2.2 Qristal benchmarks and performances

A beta version of Qristal was evaluated in July 2004 in the EQueR[4] evaluation campaign organized in France by several ministries (Ayache, 2004; Ayache, 2005). With a MRR ("Mean Reciprocal Rank"; cf. Ayache, 2004) of 0.58 for the exact answers and 0.70 for the snippets, our system ranked first out of the seven

[2] IST-1999-56416 http://www.trustsemantics.com
[3] EDC 22249, http://www.m-cast.infovide.pl
[4] http://www.technolangue.net/article61.html

Question Answering systems evaluated.

The marketed version of Qristal was evaluated during the CLEF 2005 (Laurent, 2005-2) and obtained 64% of exact answers for French to French, 39.5% from English to French and 36.5% from Portuguese to French. Once again, Qristal ranked first in this evaluation, for French engines and for all cross language systems, all pairs considered.

Since this evaluation, the resources were increased and some algorithms revised, so our last tests brought us a 70% of exacted answers and 45 % for cross language.

3 QA and IR

It is true that, intrinsically, IR engines and QA systems differ in design, objectives and processes. An IR engine is geared to deliver snippets or docs from a query, a QA system strive to deliver the exact answer to a question.

If one is to differentiate 3 key features of both systems, one of the first difference concerns the query mode : natural language for the QA systems and "Boolean like" for the IR engines. We define "Boolean like" extensively as the use of Boolean operators associated to underlying constraints induced by the word matching techniques. The table 1 gives the results of Google Desktop for natural language requests and Boolean requests (set of questions detailed below) and we can see that results with natural language requests are not so good:

rank of answers	Google snippets natural language requests	Google snippets Boolean requests	Google snippets or docs natural language requests	Google snippets or docs Boolean requests
1	4.2 %	9.7 %	7.3 %	30.6 %
1-5	6.7 %	18.5 %	14.2 %	52.1 %

Table 1. Results with Google Desktop Search on natural language and Boolean requests

This performance table shows that classical engines are not suited to answer questions in natural language. To quote Google *"A Google search is an easy, honest and objective way to find high-quality* ***websites*** *with information relevant to your search."*

The Google technology considers, at least in French, equally and of same "weight, words like, "de" or "le" and the highly semantically-loaded words of the query. This leads to a dramatic upsurge of noise in their results. Therefore, using classic engines require a good knowledge of their syntax and their underlying word matching techniques, like the necessity of grouping between quotation marks, the "noun phrases" and the expressions.

The second difference concerns what is delivered to the user. Question Answering systems deliver one or more exact answers to a question and their context whereas classical engines return snippets with links to the texts those snippets were extracted from.

The third difference relates to the dynamic and openness status of the corpora. Usually QA systems use confined or close corpora with low up-date rate, while classical IR engines are tuned to the Web queries and their reference file are continuously updated.

Qristal QA is able to deliver answers from both web-based queries and closed corpora. We were eager to apply our proposed metrics on the web-based deliveries, but unfortunately, we had not at our disposal the appropriate web reference file of questions and answers, probably impossible to elaborate considering the extremely high up-dating rate of the web pages.

Therefore we had but no choice to use a closed corpus, Google Desktop being able to manage this type of corpus (see note 1). We used the reference file of questions and answers established for EQueR.

3.1 Question Answering systems

Qristal interface mimics almost all the usual screen template of IR engine (see figure 2). It displays results in different languages, keeps the track or trace of the precedent requests, allows the user to choose the requested corpus and, if thought necessary, to make a semantic disambiguation of the question terms.

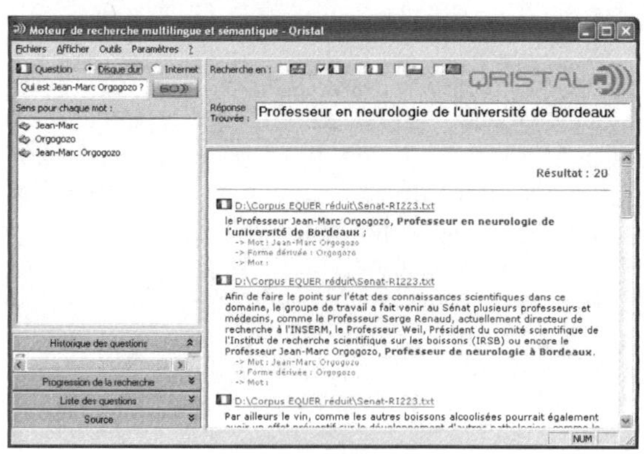

Figure 2. QRISTAL

Results (answer, sentences, links) are displayed at three levels: if an exact answer is found, it is displayed in the top right part of the window, sentences in the lower right part of the window and links on top of the sentences. Note that the words or phrases supporting the inferred answer are put in bold in the text. These words are sometimes pronouns (anaphora) and, frequently, synonyms or derivate forms of the request words.

3.2 Information Retrieval engines

Numerous Information Retrieval engines are available for closed or web-based corpora.

For our evaluation we selected the Google engine, as it is available both for a web and closed PC desktop usage (in version "Desktop Search"), although, regrettably, this beta version had a few minor defects. The snippets supplied by Google are generally fragments of sentences, sometimes with cut words, stemming from excerpts of text seeming to correspond the best to the query. All you can expect is a help in the selection of the text(s) in which is likely to be present the answer to your query rather than a pinpointed and elaborated exact answer.

3.3 Evaluation method of the performances

Corpus of requests and answers

The corpus selected for this evaluation is the corpus used for the EQueR evaluation campaign. This choice was justified by the size of the corpus (over half million texts for about 1.5 Gb) and, especially, by the fact that we have an important corpus of questions (500) with many answers and references for all these questions.

To generate a comprehensive package of tests of Question Answering systems, ELDA, organizer of the EQueR campaign, made a compilation of all the results returned by all the participants. Then, thanks to a thorough examination by several specialists (one of whom being an author of this paper), this corpus has been verified, increased and validated. In doing so, most certainly, the immense majority of the possible answers are inventoried, the great majority of the references of these answers is known[5] to the extent that this corpus of questions and answers can be automatically run, the results subsequently requiring only a reduced amount of checking.

The initial corpus of 500 questions has been reduced to 330 questions for this evaluation. In fact, the last 100 questions were only reformulations of previous questions and offered not enough interest. 30 questions concerned binary answers YES/NO and 40 questions concerned lists as answers. As Information Retrieval engines are not able to return binary or list answers, including them within the evaluation would have biased it. Finally, five questions were without any answer. They were removed by the organizers of EQueR and we also did so accordingly. For these five "no-answer"questions, Qristal systematically returned correct answers i.e. NIL, where as a classical search engine like Google would systematically return at least one answer. We decided not to include these "NIL" questions so as not further penalize the IR Google engine.

Evaluation of the "user effort"

We have two competing systems on the same corpora and a reference file with questions and answers. We need now to define the basis of their comparison.

The main comparative evaluation between the Question Answering systems and the Information Retrieval engines (Kwok, 2001) considered only the reading time while counting characters to be read to reach the answer. Knowing the delay needed to obtain the results in most Question Answering systems (McGowan, 2005), it seems necessary to take also in account this delay if we want to measure the global user effort to obtain an answer to his question.

We consider that the user wants a correct answer to his question and we consider that the answer is correct if this answer can be found in the snippet or in the text linked to the snippet for Google (to the sentence for Qristal). So we compared the quality of the systems as follows: percentage of correct answers ranked first, ranked within the five first, the ten first and the hundred first. We considered both the answer as part of the snippets or part or the snippets and documents.

For the user, the quality of the answers returned, especially in the first results page, is paramount. But, we think another item has to be taken into account: the time needed to obtain the answer. This time is the compound of three elements:

- the time to key in the question,
- the delay before the results display,
- the reading time of the snippets or sentences to reach a correct answer.

[5] a set comprising textual corpora, questions and answers is available at ELDA (http://www.elda.org/article139.html)

Addition of these three elements provides the measure of the "user effort".

Time to key in the question

This time is shorter for a “Boolean like” engine. Typing a question in Qristal needs in average nine seconds more than with the query in Google. However it supposes that the user types the Boolean like request at the same speed than a natural language request. This implies that the user is very familiar with the Google syntax. For example the question 6:

Quel âge a l'abbé Pierre ?

will be converted into Google syntax by:

"abbé Pierre" ans

This Boolean request increases the probability to obtain the effective age, not only snippets with the words "âge" and "abbé Pierre". Other example, the question 37:

Quel évènement a eu lieu le 27 décembre 1978 en Algérie ?

will be converted into Google syntax:

"27 décembre 1978" Algérie

This Boolean request is needed either words like "évènement" or "avoir lieu" will bring out more noise than correct answers.

So, we translated the complete list of question in the Google syntax in addition to the questions set in natural language. Compared results were shown on Table 1.

To measure the time necessary to enter questions, we counted the number of characters typed (always inferior in Google) and multiplied this number by an average speed of 150 characters by minute. We know that a professional typist types at a speed of 300 to 400 characters per minute, so our chosen speed corresponds to a user keying in with two fingers. The following table gives the numbers of characters and the times for the two systems:

	characters	mean time
Qristal	49.1	19.6 seconds
Google Desktop	27.2	10.9 seconds

Table 3: mean time of question entering

Delay to display the results

This is the elapsed time between the click on the button "OK" and the display of the results. Note here that, strangely, Google Desktop has a response time distinctly bigger than the response time of Google on the Web, especially when the request contains a group of words between quotes.

Reading time to reach one answer

To fix a reading speed, we tested several users. An average speed of 40 characters by second (2 400 characters per minute, or also 400 words per minute) seems a fair measure. It corresponds to a reader with a higher-education background, according to Richaudeau, 1977. While making these tests, we noted that, if the user knows the answer, the reading speed of both the snippets and texts would increase to 100 characters per second (6 000 characters per minute, or 1 000 words per minute). Even if very few questions have an obvious answer, we decided to calculate the reading times with both speeds of 40 characters per second and 100 characters per second.

The speed of 100 characters per second will however be considered as a superior limit that favours clearly Google where the snippets, constituted by fragments of sentences, sometimes fragments of words, are more difficult and longer to read than the sentences returned by Qristal.

4 Results of the benchmark

4.1 Evaluation on the 330 questions

For the 330 questions of the evaluation, results are:

Answer rank	Google Desktop snippets	Qristal snippets	Google Desktop snippets or docs	Qristal snippets or docs
Exact answer		69.7 %		69.7 %
1 or exact	9.7 %	81.8 %	30.6 %	86.7 %
1-5	18.5 %	88.2 %	51.9 %	94.5 %
1-10	21.5 %	88.8 %	58.5 %	96.1 %
1-100	27.0 %	90.9 %	70.0 %	98.5 %
Not found	73.0 %	9.1 %	30. 0 %	1.5 %

Table 4: Percentage of correct answers / 330

Qristal returns an exact answer for nearly 70% of questions and a correct answer is returned as exact answer or in the first sentence for 82% of the 330 questions. This has to be compared with the 10% of answer found in first position by Google Desktop. If we consider the snippets and the documents, Qristal returns a correct answer in first rank for 86% of the questions and Google in more than 30%.

These results give a clear advantage to the Question Answering system on the Information Retrieval engine. This superiority in quality exists also in quantity. Here is the table of user efforts to obtain a correct answer:

	Google Desktop	Qristal
Type the question	10.9 s	19.6 s
Display results	3.0 s	2.1 s
Reading 40 char/second	59.3 s	7.1 s
Reading 100 char/second	23.7 s	2.8 s
Display results + Reading 40 characters/second	62.3 s	9.2 s
Display results + Reading 100 characters/second	26.7 s	4.9 s
Type the question + Display results + Reading 40 c./second	73.2 s	28.8 s
Type the question + Display results + Reading 100 c./second	37.6 s	24.5 s

Table 5: Mean times compared for the two systems (on 330 questions)

It appears that the time to type down the question in Qristal is nearly 9 seconds longer than with Google. The elapsed time before display is similar. On the other hand, as Google gives a correct answer in a higher rank or in a document, not a snippet, the number of characters to be read before reaching an answer is finally more important. Finally, if we consider the average reading speed of 40 characters per second, Qristal needs in average 29 seconds against 73 seconds, in other words the user effort to obtain a good answer is 2.5 times higher with Google than with Qristal.

If we don't take into account the time to enter the question, Google requires a user effort 6 to 7 time higher than Qristal to reach an answer. This comparison would be effective in the case of voice-based submitted query. In that case, the acquisition of the question would become more difficult according to the syntax of the Boolean engine ("open the quotes", "close the quotes"...)

4.2 Evaluation on 231 questions

Looking carefully at each answer returned by Google Desktop, we discovered that it ignored some texts or, more exactly, some parts of texts, especially the end of these texts. The help pages of this software point out this "bug" :

However, if you're searching for a word within the file, please note that Google Desktop searches only about the first 10,000 words. In a few cases, Google Desktop may index slightly fewer words to save space in your search index and on your hard drive.[6]

Of course this default impacted on the results and the comparisons. Thus, we decided, in a second iteration of this evaluation, to consider only the 231 questions where Google Desktop found at least one correct answer. Google Desktop found no answer with those 99 (330-231) removed questions for two main reasons. Firstly, as it doesn't manage a full indexation of documents. Secondly, as some complex questions like "why" or "how" questions often lead it to silence on this evaluation.

This selection of 231 questions favours Google Desktop but it allows a more accurate comparison. Here are the results for those 231 questions:

Scale	Google Desktop bribes	Qristal bribes	Google Desktop bribes ou docs	Qristal bribes ou docs
Exact answer		73.6 %		73.6 %
1	13.9 %	89.6 %	43.7 %	90.9 %
1-5	26.4 %	94.8 %	74.0 %	97.4 %
1-10	30.7 %	94.8 %	83.5 %	97.8 %
1-100	38.5 %	96.1 %	100.0 %	99.6 %
Not found		3.9 %		0.4 %

Table 6: Number of answers and percentages / 231

The corpus of 231 questions is thus "easier" than that of 325 questions. This confirms the score of Qristal for the exact answers: 73.6% versus 69.7%, and the score for the correct answer in first rank: 89.6% versus 81.8%. But the results of Google are of course better: 13.9% in the first snippet against 9.7%, 43.7% in the first snippet or the first document, against 30.6%.

However the advantage of the QA system over the IR engine is clear in terms of quality, especially if we consider only the snippets. This advantage is also clear for the user effort, even if any of the answer not found by Qristal penalizes this system as the reading time of this question is the consolidation of all reading times of all the snippets displayed for this question!

	Google	Qristal
Type the question	10.1 s	18.7 s
Display results	3.5 s	2.0 s
Reading 40 char/second	28.4 s	3.3 s
Reading 100 char/second	11.4 s	1.3 s
Display results + Reading 40 char/second	31.9 s	5.3 s
Display results + Reading 100 char/second	14.9 s	3.3 s
Type + Display results + Reading 40 char/second	42.0 s	23.9 s
Type + Display results + Reading 100 char/second	24.9 s	21.9 s

Table 7: Mean times compared for the two systems (on 231 questions)

[6] http://desktop.google.com/support/bin/answer.py?answer=24755&topic=209

The mean times of question entering and displaying results are nearly the same for those 231 questions than for the 325 questions. But, because Google Desktop finds an answer to all questions, the reading time before a correct answer is, in that case, reduced for Google.

The mean times of question entering and displaying results are nearly the same for those 231 questions than for the 325 questions. But, because Google Desktop finds an answer to all questions, the reading time before a correct answer is, in that case, reduced for Google.

Finally, with an average reading speed of 40 characters by second, the user effort is two times higher with Google Desktop than it is with Qristal. And if we don't take into account the time to type in the question, the user effort with Google is 6 times higher than with Qristal.

Using the same presentation than Kwok, 2001, the following graph gives the compared results of the two systems. On Y-axis is the number of correct answers and in X-axis the number of characters read, for the 231 questions:

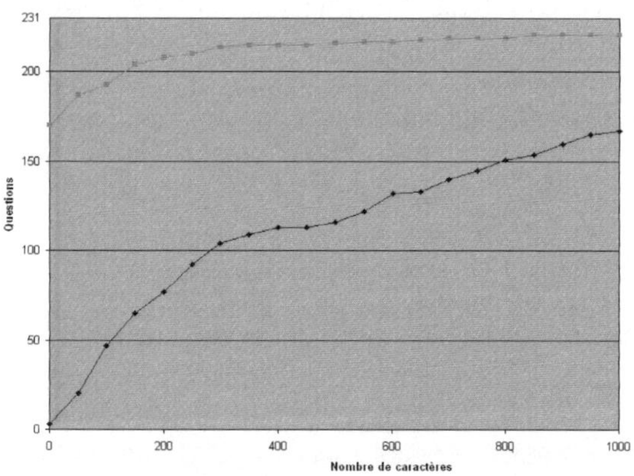

Figure 8 : number of correct answers by characters

The interest of Question Answering systems is particularly noticeable at the beginning of the graph, seeing that Qristal displays a correct answer as exact answer at the top of the screen in more than 70% of the questions while Google Desktop needs to read about 1000 characters in the snippets and in the documents to obtain a similar success rate.

4.3 Comparison by type of question(s)

The above statistics concern all types of queries. In fact, 25 questions wait a definition, the others being factual requests. The following table of the 231 questions corpus gives the results for these two categories:

Answer rank	Google snippets	Qristal snippets	Google snippets or docs	Qristal snippets or docs
Exact definition		64.0 %		64.0 %
Definition in rank 1	32.0 %	88.0 %	48.0 %	92.0 %
Definition in rank 1-5	52.0 %	96.0 %	68.0 %	100 %
Exact factual		74.8 %		74.8 %
Factual rank 1	11.7 %	89.8 %	43.2 %	90.8 %
Factual rank 1-5	23.3 %	94.7 %	74.8 %	97.6 %

Table 9 : Percentages of answers by type of questions

The only significant gap in these results is that Google provides better results for definitions (32% of correct answers in the first snippet against 12% for the factual questions).

We also looked at the questions beginning by "comment" ("how"), but we excluded those beginning by "comment s'appelle" ("how is called") or "comment est mort" ("how did somebody die"), i.e. 16 questions (3, 50, 59, 90, 93, 117, 148, 154, 165, 196, 199, 234, 247, 249, 263, 295). The results are :

Rank	Google snippets	Qristal snippets	Google snippets or docs	Qristal snippets or docs
Exact		25.0 %		25.0 %
1	0.0 %	56.3 %	18.8 %	56.3 %
1-5	6.3 %	68.8 %	25.0 %	81.3 %
1-10	6.3 %	68.8 %	25.0 %	81.3 %
1-100	12.5 %	68.8 %	37.5 %	81.3 %
Not found	87.5 %	31.2 %	62.5 %	18.7 %

Table 10: Percentage of correct answers for questions beginning by "comment" ("how")

These results are not satisfying for any of the two systems but Qristal displays a correct answer in 9 cases on 16, versus 0 for Google Desktop. This underlines that the Question Answering systems are more successful when the queries are not purely factual requests. Most certainly this could be caused by the fact that those questions require a deeper analysis.

A closer examination of factual questions revealed that the most difficult questions for the Information Retrieval engines are the questions about location. For example Google Desktop finds the country related to the Vilvorde town only at the 23rd rank, and the country related to Johannesburg is given only at the 13th rank; the region of Cancale is displayed at the 18th rank;

and the department (county) where is located Annemasse only at the 23rd rank.

More generally, a search engine finds answers more easily when these answers contain the words of the query. For example, to the query 252 ("*À quelle peine fut condamné Jean-Marie Villemin le 16 décembre 1993?*" [*"What was the sentence received by Jean-Marie Villemin on 16 December 1993 ?"]*), Google Desktop does not find any answer because the acceptable answers "cinq ans de prison" (five years of prison) or "cinq années d'emprisonnement" (a five-year prison sentence) does not contain, in French, any word of the query. Similarly the search engine has many difficulties to display the development of acronyms like those of the question 141 ("*Que signifie CGT?*" [*"What is the significance of CGT?"]*), or of the question 319 ("*Qu'est-ce que l'EEE?" ["What is EEE?"]*). Because the answers are developments of these capital letters which are not so frequent, except when the acronym is rare, as in this case the acronym is often followed or preceded by his significance, like for the questions 327 ("*Qu'est-ce que le Cermoc ?" ["What is Cermoc?"]*) or 330 ("*Qu'est-ce que l'OACI ?" [What is OACI?"]*). For these two questions, Google Desktop returns the correct answer in the first snippet.

5 Perspectives

The evaluation was designed in such fair way to take into account all the differences between the Information Retrieval engines and the Question Answering systems.

We made all possible efforts not to favour the QA systems and avoid non equitable comparison. For example, the evaluation includes the requests to Google Desktop made with the most sophisticated achievable query syntax to generate a return of the best answers, knowing that if they were keyed in as for the natural language requests, their success rate would have dropped considerably (see Table 1).

It is most unlikely that one is able to formulate queries in Boolean like style as quickly as in NL questions. Conversely, for a same given number of characters, reading Google snippets requires most likely far more time than reading complete NL sentences. However, despite all these metrical choices more favourable to the classical search engine, the Question Answering system obtains better results with regard to the quality of the answers and to the user effort.

If we were able to compare the Web versions of Google and Qristal, the results would be probably different.

First, because Qristal uses the search engines as a meta-engine without any indexation. Next, because GoogleWeb is really faster at displaying the results from the Web than Google Desktop. At last because the redundancy, due to the large volume of indexed pages on the Web, allows the implementation of some very successful techniques.

For example it may happen that you find the questions in natural language followed by their answers inside Web pages and this in such a way that asking a request in natural language in Google, you can obtain sometimes a very pertinent answer. To the question "*Pourquoi le ciel est bleu?*" (*"Why the sky is blue?"*) or to the question "*Pourquoi la mer est bleue?*" (*"Why the sea is blue?"*), Google Web returns in first rank snippets and documents very accurately.

However the analysis of the documents and contained answers permit to the Question Answering systems to return more accurate answers. For example, with the request "*capitale anglaise*" ("*English capital*"), Google returns a lot of snippets containing the phrase "*capitale anglaise*" ("*English capital*") but not the word Londres or London in these snippets. In an Information Retrieval engine the answers are very often less justified by the context than it is the case with Question Answering systems. This is because the snippets group essentially words contained in the query. For example, to the question 26 ("*Qui a écrit Germinal?*" ["*Who wrote Germinal?*"], converted in Google syntax by : "*auteur Germinal*" ["writer Germinal"]), the search engine returns "Émile Zola" in the second snippet but the snippet "*L'exposition "Emile Zola, photographe" fait escale*" (*The exhibition "Emile Zola, photograph" stops at)* would be considered as an answer out of its context and non receivable within a campaign like TREC, even if we can read in the text : "*L'auteur de "Germinal", l'écrivain français Emile Zola (1840-1902), était aussi un photographe de talent*" (*"The author of Germinal, the writer Emile Zola (1840-1902), was also a talented photograph"*). We could almost say that the classical search engines return far better results when the user already knows the answer to his query.

A complete compared benchmark and exhaustive evaluation of search engines and question answering systems needs to be made on the Web.

The evaluation method described above could be applied but, knowing the difficulty to validate a Web corpus of answers, specially the difficulty to keep it referentially constant, the effort to estimate the quality of the returned answers would be far much enormous than the one engaged for this evaluation on a closed corpus.

6 Conclusion

We described a metrical method to compare Question Answering systems and Information Retrieval engines on a hard disk-based corpus. Applied to our system Qristal and to the search engine Google Desktop, this method shows that the improvements due to question answering systems, especially in terms of user effort, are both qualitative and quantitative. Taking into account or not the query keying time, the question answering system is 2 to 6 times faster than the Information Retrieval engine.

This evaluation, made almost automatically with the corpus EQueR, focuses mainly on factual or definition types of requests which defines the majority of the requests concerned in the QA system evaluation campaigns. On more complex questions, like those beginning by "comment" ("how..."), the QA systems obtained less satisfying results than for factual questions but, on this type of questions, the search engines like Google proved to be also less accurate. A more exhaustive and thorough study on these types of requests or on questions beginning by "pourquoi" ("why") would possibly confirm these results, although here only a few questions were of these types.

At last, a similar metrics and applied evaluation remain to be endeavoured on a web-based corpus despite the entailing difficulties.

References

Amaral C., Laurent D., Martins A., Mendes A., Pinto C. (2004), Design & Implementation of a Semantic Search Engine for Portuguese, In Proceedings of the Fourth Conference on Language Resources and Evaluation.

Amaral C., Figueira H., Martins A., Mendes A., Mendes P., Pinto C., (2005) Priberam's Question Answering System for Portuguese. In Working Notes for the CLEF 2005 Workshop, 21-23 September, Vienna, Austria

Ayache C., Choukri K., Grau B. (2004) Campagne EVALDA/EQueR Évaluation en Question-Réponse. http://www.technolangue.net/IMG/pdf/rapport_EQUER_1.2.pdf

Ayache C., Grau B., Vilnat A., (2005) Campagne d'évaluation EQueR-EVALDA : Évaluation en question-réponse. In TALN & RECITAL 2005, Tome 2 - Ateliers et tutoriels, pp. 63-72

Buchholz S., (2002) Open-Domain Question Answering on the World Wide Web. Tutorial, http://tcc.itc.it/research/textec/topics/ question-answering/Tut-Bucholtz.html.

Kwok C., Etzioni O., Weld D.S., (2001) Scaling Question Answering to the Web. In Proceedings International WWW Conference(10), Hong-Kong

Laurent D., Varone M., Amaral C., Fuglewicz P. (2004) Multilingual Semantic and Cognitive Search Engine for Text Retrieval Using Semantic Technologies, First International Workshop on Proofing Tools and Language Technologies, Patras, Grèce.

Laurent D., Séguéla P., Nègre S., (2005-1) QRISTAL, système de Questions-Réponses. In TALN & RECITAL 2005, Tome 1 - Conférences principales, pp. 53-62

Laurent D., Séguéla P., Nègre S., (2005-2) Cross-Lingual Question Answering using Qristal for CLEF 2005. In Working Notes for the CLEF 2005 Workshop, 21-23 September, Vienna, Austria

McGowan K., (2005) Emma : A Natural Language Question Answering System for umich.edu. http://www-personal.umich.edu/~clunis/emma/

Radev D.R., Qi H., Wu H., Fan W., (2002) Evaluating Web-based Question Answering Systems. In the Proceedings of the 11th WWW conference, Hawaii.

Richaudeau F., Gauquelin M. et F., (1977) La méthode complète de lecture rapide "Richaudeau", éd. Retz-CEPL, Paris.

Vallin A. Giampiccolo D., AunimoL., Ayache C., Osenova P., Peñas A., de Rijke M., Sacaleanu B., Santos D., Sutcliffe R. (2005) Overview of the CLEF 2005 Multilingual Question Answering Track. In Working Notes for the CLEF 2005 Workshop, 21-23 September, Vienna, Austria

Voorhees E.M., (2005) Overview of the TREC 2004 Question Answering Track. In Proceedings of the Thirteenth Text REtrieval Conference (TREC 2004).

The Affect of Machine Translation on the Performance of Arabic-English QA System

Azzah Al-Maskari
Dept. of Information Studies,
University of Sheffield,
Sheffield, S10 2TN, UK
lip05aaa@shef.ac.uk

Mark Sanderson
Dept. of Information Studies,
University of Sheffield,
Sheffield, S10 2TN, UK
m.sanderson@shef.ac.uk

Abstract

The aim of this paper is to investigate how much the effectiveness of a Question Answering (QA) system was affected by the performance of Machine Translation (MT) based question translation. Nearly 200 questions were selected from TREC QA tracks and ran through a question answering system. It was able to answer 42.6% of the questions correctly in a monolingual run. These questions were then translated manually from English into Arabic and back into English using an MT system, and then re-applied to the QA system. The system was able to answer 10.2% of the translated questions. An analysis of what sort of translation error affected which questions was conducted, concluding that factoid type questions are less prone to translation error than others.

1 Introduction

Increased availability of on-line text in languages other than English and increased multi-national collaboration have motivated research in Cross-Language Information Retrieval (CLIR). The goal of CLIR is to help searchers find relevant documents when their query terms are chosen from a language different from the language in which the documents are written. Multilinguality has been recognized as an important issue for the future of QA (Burger et al. 2001). The multilingual QA task was introduced for the first time in the Cross-Language Evaluation Forum CLEF-2003.

According to the Global Reach web site (2004), shown in Figure 1, it could be estimated that an English speaker has access to around 23 times more digital documents than an Arabic speaker. One can conclude from the given information shown in the Figure that cross-language is potentially very useful when the required information is not available in the users' language.

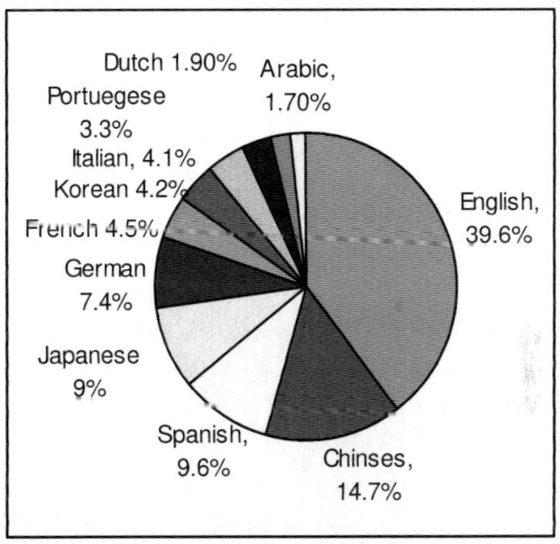

Figure 1: Online language Population (March, 2004)

The goal of a QA system is to find answers to questions in a large collection of documents. The overall accuracy of a QA system is directly affected by its ability to correctly analyze the questions it receives as input, a Cross Language Question Answering (CLQA) system will be sensitive to any errors introduced during question translation. Many researchers criticize the MT-based CLIR approach. The reason for their criticism mostly stem from the fact that the current translation quality of MT is poor, in addition MT system are expensive to develop and their application degrades the retrieval efficiency due to the cost of the linguistic analysis.

This paper investigates the extent to which MT error affects QA accuracy. It is divided as follows: in section 2 relevant previous work on cross-language retrieval is described, section 3 explains the experimental approach which includes the procedure and systems employed, it also discuss the results obtained, section 4 draws conclusions and future research on what improvements need to be done for MT systems.

2 Related Research

CLIR is an active area, extensive research on CLIR and the effects of MT on QA systems' retrieval effectiveness has been conducted. Lin and Mitamua (2004) point out that the quality of translation is fully dependent upon the MT system employed.

Perret (2004) proposed a question answering system designed to search French documents in response to French queries. He used automatic translation resources to translate the original queries from (Dutch, German, Italian, Portuguese, Spanish, English and Bulgarian) and reports the performance level in the monolingual task was 24.5% dropping to 17% in the bilingual task. A similar experiment was conducted by Plamondon and Foster (2003) on TREC questions and measured a drop of 44%, and in another experiment using Babelfish, the performance dropped even more, 53%. They believe that CLEF questions were easier to process because they did not include definition questions, which are harder to translate. Furthermore, Plamondon and Foster (2004) compare the cross language version of their Quantum QA system with the monolingual English version on CLEF questions and note the performance of a cross-language system (French questions and English documents) was 28% lower than the monolingual system using IBM1 translation.

Tanev et al. (2004) note that DIOGENE system, which relies on the Multi-WordNet, performs 15% better in the monolingual (Italian-Italian) than cross-language task (Italian-English). In Magnini et al.'s (2004) report for the year 2003, the average performance of correct answers on monolingual tasks was 41% and 25% in the bilingual tasks. In addition in the year 2004, the average accuracy in the monolingual tasks was 23.7% and 14.7% in bilingual tasks.

As elucidated above, much research has been conducted to evaluate the effectiveness of QA systems in a cross language platform by employing MT systems to translate the queries from the source language to the target language. However, most of them are focused on European language pairs. To our knowledge, only one past example of research has investigated the performance of a cross-language Arabic-English QA system Rosso et al (2005). The QA system used by Rosso et al (2005) is based on a system reported in Del Castillo (2004). Their experiment was carried out using the question corpus of the CLEF-2003 competition. They used questions in English and compared the answers with those obtained after the translation back into English from an Arabic question corpus which was manually translated. For the Arabic-English translation process, an automatic machine translator, the TARJIM Arabic-English machine translation system, was used. Rosso el al reported a decrease of QA accuracy by more than 30% which was caused by the translation process.

Work in the Rosso paper was limited to a single QA and MT system and also did not analyze types of errors or how those errors affected different types of QA questions. Therefore, it was decided to conduct further research on MT systems and its affect on the performance in QA systems. This paper presents an extension on the previous mentioned study, but with more diverse ranges of TREC data set using different QA system and different MT system.

3 Experimental Approach

To run this experiment, 199 questions were randomly compiled from the TREC QA track, namely from TREC-8, TREC-9, TREC-11, TREC-2003 and TREC-2004, to be run through AnswerFinder, the results of which are discussed in section 3.1. The selected 199 English TREC questions were translated into Arabic by one of the authors (who is an Arabic speaker), and then fed into Systran to translate them into English. The analysis of translation is discussed in detail in section 3.2.

3.1 Performance of AnswerFinder

The 199 questions were run over AnswerFinder; divided as follows: 92 factoid questions, 51 definition questions and 56 list questions. The answers were manually assessed following an assessment scheme similar to the answer categories in iCLEF 2004:

- *Correct:* if the answer string is valid and supported by the snippets

- *Non-exact:* if the answer string is missing some information, but the full answer is found in the snippets.
- *Wrong:* if the answer string and the snippets are missing important information or both the answer string and the snippets are wrong compared with the answer key.
- *No answer:* if the system does not return any answer at all.

Table 1 provides an overall view, the system correctly answered 42.6% of these questions, whereas 25.8% wrongly, 23.9% no answer and 8.1% non-exactly. Table 2 illustrates AnswerFinder' abilities to answer each type of these questions separately.

Answer Type	
Correct	42.6%
Non exact	8.1%
Wrong	25.8%
No Answer	23.9%

Table 1. Overall view of AnswerFinder Monolingual Accuracy

	Factoid	Definition	List
Correct	63	6	15
Not exact	1	6	9
Wrong	22	15	13
No answer	6	23	18

Table 2. Detail analysis of AnswerFinder Performance-monolingual run

To measure the performance of AnswerFinder, recall (ratio of relevant items retrieved to all relevant items in a collection) and precision (the ratio of relevant items retrieved to all retrieved items) were calculated. Thus, recall and precision and F-measure for AnswerFinder are, 0.51 and 0.76, 0.6 respectively.

3.2 Systran Translation

Most of the errors noticed during the translation process were of the following types: wrong transliteration, wrong word sense, wrong word order, and wrong pronoun translations. Table 3 lists Systran's translation errors to provide correct transliteration 45.7%, wrong word senses (key word) 31%, wrong word order 25%, and wrong translation of pronoun 13.5%.

Below is a discussion of Systran' translation accuracy and the problems that occurred during translation of the TREC QA track questions.

Type of Translation Error	Percentage
Wrong Transliteration	45.7%
Wrong Sense	31%
Wrong Word Order	25%
Wrong Pronoun	13.5%

Table 3. Types of Translation Errors

Wrong Transliteration

Wrong transliteration is the most common error that encountered during translation. Transliteration is the process of replacing words in the source language with their phonetic equivalent in the target language. Al-Onaizan and Knight (2002) state that transliterating names from Arabic into English is a non-trivial task due to the differences in their sound and writing system. Also, there is no one-to-one correspondence between Arabic sounds and English sounds. For example P and B are both mapped to the single Arabic letter "ب"; Arabic "ح" and "ه "are mapped into English H.

Original text	Who is Aga[1] Khan[2]?
Arabic version	من يكون[1] اجا[2] خان؟
Translation (wrong)	From [EEjaa][1] betrayed[2]?

Table 4. Incorrect use of translation when transliteration should have been used

Original text	Who is Hasan[1] Rohani[2]
Arabic version	من يكون[1] حسن[2] روحاني؟
Translation (wrong)	From spiritual[2] goodness[1] is?

Table 5. Wrong translation of person's name

Transliteration mainly deals with proper names errors when MT doesn't recognize them as a proper name and translates them instead of transliterating them. Systran produced 91 questions (45.7%) with wrong transliteration. It translated some names literally, especially those with a descriptive meaning. Table 4 provides an example of such cases where "Aga" was wrongly transliterated; and "khan" was translated to "betray" where it should have been transliterated. This can also be seen in table 5; "Hassan Rohani" was translated literally as "Spiritual goodness".

Wrong Word Sense

Wrong translation of words can occur when a single word can have different senses according to the context in which the word is used. Word sense problems are commoner in Arabic than in a language like English as Arabic vowels (written as diacritics) are largely unwritten in most texts.

Systran translated 63 questions (31.2%) with at least one wrong word sense, 25% of them could have been resolved by adding diacritics. Table 6 illustrates an error resulting from Systran's failure to translate words correctly even after diacritics have been added; the term "عِلم النّفس" (psychology) was wrongly translated as "flag of breath". The Arabic form is a compound phrase; however Systran translated each word individually even after diacritics were added.

Original text	Who was the father of psychology?
Arabic version	مَن أب عِلم النّفس
Translation (wrong)	From father flag of the breath?

Table 6. Example of incorrect translation due to incorrect sense choice

These errors can occur when a single word can have different senses according to the con-text in which the word is used. They also occur due to the diacritization in Arabic language. Arabic writing involves diacritization (vowel), which is largely ignored in modern texts. Ali (2003) gives a good example that can make an English speaker grasp the complexity caused by dropping Arabic diacritization. Suppose that vowels are dropped from an English word and the result is 'sm'. The possibilities of the original word are: some, same, sum, and semi.

Systran translated 63 questions out of 199 (31.2%) with wrong word sense, 25% of them can be resolved by adding diacritization.

Wrong Word Order

Word order errors occurred when the translated words were in order that made no sense and this problem produced grammatically ill formed sentences that the QA system was unable to process. Systran translated 25% of the questions with wrong word orders which lead to the construction of ungrammatical questions. Table 7 shows an example of wrong word order.

Original text	What are the names of the space shuttles?
Arabic version	ما أسماء المكوك الفضائي؟
Translation (wrong)	What space name of the shuttle?

Table 7. Wrong word order

Wrong Pronoun

Systran frequently translated the pronoun "هو" to "air" in place of "him" or "it" as shown in table 8. Table 9 shows an example pronoun problems; the pronoun "ها" is translated into "her", instead of "it", which refers to "building" in this case.

Original text	Who is Colin Powell?
Arabic version	مَن هُو كولن باول؟
Translation (wrong)	From Collin Powell air?

Table 8. Wrong translation of "*who*"

Original text	What buildings had Frank designed?
Arabic version	ما المباني التي صممها فرانك؟
Translation (wrong)	What the buildings which designed her Frank?

Table 9. wrong pro-drop of translation of "it"

It has been observed that Systran translation errors exhibited some clear regularities for certain questions as might be expected from a rule-based system. As shown in tables 2,3,4,7 the term "مَنْ" was translated to "from" instead of "who". This problem is related to the recognition of diacritization.

Arabic Word	English Translation Returned	Expected
حجم	Big	size
أطول	Tall, big	long
الأرض	Ground	earth
يوجد	Create	locate
دول	Nation	country
أبعد	Far	distance
أكثر	Many	most, much

Table 10. List of wrong key word returned by Systran

The evaluator observed that Systran' propensity to produce some common wrong sense translations which lead to change the meaning of the questions, table 10 shows some of these common sense translation.

3.3 The Effectiveness of AnswerFinder combined with Systran' Translation

After translating the 199 questions using Systran, they were passed to AnswerFinder. Figure 2 illustrates the system's abilities to answer the original and the translated questions; AnswerFinder was initially able to answer 42.6% of the questions while after translation, its accuracy to return correct answers dropped to 10.2%. Its failure to return any answer increased by 35.5% (from 23.9% to 59.4%); in addition, non-exact answers decreased by 6.6% while wrong answers increased by 3.6% (from 25.4% to 28.9%).

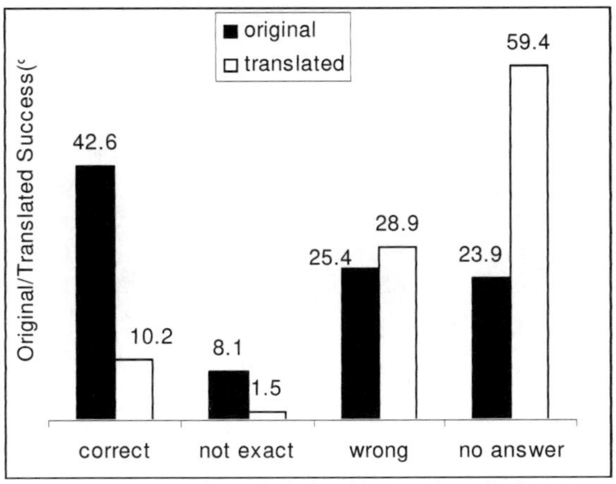

Figure 2. Answering Original/Translated Questions (%)

AnswerFinder was able to answer 23 translated questions out of 199. Out of these 23 questions, 12 were correctly translated and 11 exhibited some translation errors. Looking closely at the 12 corrected translated question (shown in table 11), 9 of them are of the factoid type, one of definition type and two of the list type. And by investigating the other 11 questions that exhibited some translation errors (shown in table 12), it can be noticed that 9 of them are factoid and 2 are list types. Our assumption for Systran' ability to translate factoid questions more than definition and list questions is that they exhibited less pronouns, in contrast to definition and list questions where many proper names were included.

In total, Systran has significantly reduced AnswerFinder's ability to return correct answers by 32.4%. Table 13 shows recall, precision and F-measure before and after translation, the value of recall before translation is 0.51 and after translation has dropped down to 0.12. Similarly, the precision value has gone down from 0.76 to 0.41, accordingly the F-measure also dropped down from 0.6 to 0.2. Altogether, in multilingual retrieval task precision and recall are 40.6% and 30%, respectively, below the monolingual retrieval task.

Question Type	Correctly translated	Correctly answered after translation
Factoid	(9/92)	(19/92)
Defn.	(1/51)	(0/51)
List	(2/56)	(3/56)
Total	12	13

Table 11. Types of questions translated and answered correctly in the bilingual run

Translation Error Type	Question Type
Word Sense	4 factoid
Word Order	2 factoid, 2 list
Diacritics	2 factoid
Transliteration	1 factoid
Total	11 questions

Table 12. Classification of wrongly translated questions but correctly answered

Effectiveness measure	Before Translation	After Translation
Recall	0.51	0.12
Precision	0.76	0.41
F-measure	0.6	0.2

Table 13. Effectiveness measures of AnswerFinder

4 Conclusions

Systran was used to translate 199 TREC questions from Arabic into English. We have scrutinized the quality of Systran's translation through out this paper. Several translation errors appeared during translations which are of the type: wrong transliteration, wrong word sense, wrong word order and wrong pronoun. The translated questions were fed into AnswerFinder, which had a big impact on its accuracy in returning correct answers. AnswerFinder was seriously affected by the relatively poor output of Systran; its effectiveness was degraded by 32.4%. This conclusion confirms Rosso et al (2005) findings using different QA system, different test sets and different machine translation system. Our results validate their results which they concluded that translation of the queries from Arabic into English has reduced the accuracy of QA system by more than 30%.

We recommend using multiple MT to give a wider range of translation to choose from, hence, correct translation is more likely to appear in multiple MT systems than in a single MT system. However, it is essential to note that in some cases MT systems may all disagree with one another in providing correct translation or they may agree on the wrong translation.

It should also be borne in mind that some keywords are naturally more important than others, so in a question-answering setting it is more important to translate them correctly. Some keywords may not be as important, and some keywords due to the incorrect analysis of the English question sentence by the Question Analysis module, may even degrade the translation and question-answering performance.

We believe there are ways to avoid the MT errors that discussed previously (i.e. wrong transliteration, wrong word senses, wrong word order, and wrong translation of pronoun). Below are some suggestions to overcome such problems:

- One solution is to make some adjustments (Pre or Post- processing) to the question translation process to minimize the effects of translation by automatically correcting some regular errors using a regular written expression.

- Another possible solution is to try building an interactive MT system by providing users more than one translation to pick the most accurate one, we believe this will offer a great help in resolving word sense problem. This is more suit-able for expert users of a language.

In this paper, we have presented the errors associated with machine translation which indicates that the current state of MT is not very reliable for cross language QA. Much work has been done in the area of machine translation for CLIR; however, the evaluation often focuses on retrieval effectiveness rather than translation correctness.

Acknowledgement

We would like to thank EU FP6 project BRICKS (IST-2002-2.3.1.12) and Ministry of Manpower, Oman, for partly funding this study. Thanks are also due to Mark Greenwood for helping us with access to his AnswerFinder system.

References

Burger, J., Cardie, C., Chaudhri, V., Gaizauskas, R., Harabagiu, S., Israel, D., Jacquemin, C., Lin,C., Maiorano, S., Miller, G., Moldovan, D., Ogden, B., Prager, J., Riloff, E., Singhal, A., Shrihari, R., Strzalkowski, T., Voorhees, E., Weishedel, R., (2001) Issues, Tasks and Program Structures to Roadmap Research in Question & Answering (Q&A). *Technical report, National Institute of Standards and Technology (NIST)*

Del Castillo, M., Montes y Gómez, M., and Villaseñor, L. (2004) QA on the web: A preliminary study for Spanish language. *Proceedings of the 5th Mexican International Conference on Computer Science (ENC04)*, Colima, Mexico.

Hull, D. A., and Grefenstette, G. (1996) Querying across languages: a dictionary-based approach to multilingual information retrieval. *Research and Development in Information Retrieval*, pp46-57.

Lin, F., & Mitamura, T. (2004) Keyword Translation from English to Chinese for Multilingual QA. In: *The 6th Conference of the Association for Machine Translation in the Americas (AMTA-2004)*

Magnini, B., Vallin, A., Ayache C., Erbach, G., Peñas, A., Rijke, M. Rocha, P., Simov, K., Sutcliffe, R. (2004) Overview of the CLEF 2004 Multi-lingual Question Answering Track. In: *Proceedings of CLEF 2004*

Perrot, L. (2004). Question Answering system for the French Language. In: *Proceedings of CLEF 2004*

Plamondon, L. and Foster, G. (2003) Quantum, a French/English Cross-Language Question Answering System. *Proceedings of CLEF 2003*

Tanev, H., Negri, M., Magnini, B., Kouylekov, M. (2004) The Diogenes Question Answering System at CLEF-2004. *Proceedings of CLEF 2004*

Yaser Al-Onaizan and Kevin Knight. (2002) Translating Named Entities Using Monolingual and Bilingual Resources. In: *Proceedings of the ACL Workshop on Computational Approaches to Semitic Languages*

Cross-Cutting Aspects of Cross-Language Question Answering Systems

Bogdan Sacaleanu
Language Technology Group
DFKI GmbH
Saarbrücken, Germany
bogdan@dfki.de

Günter Neumann
Language Technology Group
DFKI GmbH
Saarbrücken, Germany
neumann@dfki.de

Abstract

We describe on-going work in the development of a cross-language question-answering framework for the open domain. An overview of the framework is being provided, some details on the important concepts of a flexible framework are presented and two cross-cutting aspects (cross-linguality and credibility) for question-answering systems are up for discussion.

1 Introduction

Different projects, different evaluation forums, different tasks, different languages, different document collections, different question types, different answer processing strategies … Anyone familiar with all these concepts knows the complexity and what a daunting prospect of developing a QA-System easily adaptable to ever changing requirements this might be. We have started off with a "prototype-and-go" approach, trying to keep pace with the emergence of new tasks and managing the scarcity of your time and of your resources, to realize later on that what we had is a bunch of prototypes very tuned to their task requirements. Trying to adapt them to new requirements seemed often more difficult then starting off with a new one. Therefore we started looking for an alternative, which should be more flexible and should allow us to cover much more requirements' variations; in other words we were considering putting together a Question Answering framework.

In the rest of the paper we will shortly overview the components of such a framework and will describe the relevant aspects of the solution offered for each of them, aspects that should account for a large variety of question types, document collections and answer processing techniques, as well as for several languages. We will continue with a discussion of two issues that cut across several components of the framework, namely: cross-linguality and answer credibility, and will conclude by shortly naming the domains of usage for the framework and future work.

2 Framework Overview

Based on an existing set of cross-language Question Answering prototypes developed for different requirements, we began by looking for the commonalities among them. Following is a list of `reusable` components that might be considered as a starting point in defining a QA framework (see Figure 1).

Several components along the work-flow of a typical QA system were identified: a `Unit Alignment` component in cross-language environments and a `Query Expansion` component for the Question Analysis task; a `Unit Processor` and a `Query Generator` component for the Information Retrieval task; a `Mention Chain` component for the Answer Extraction task and a `Scoring Strategy` for the Answer Selection task. (see Figure 1)

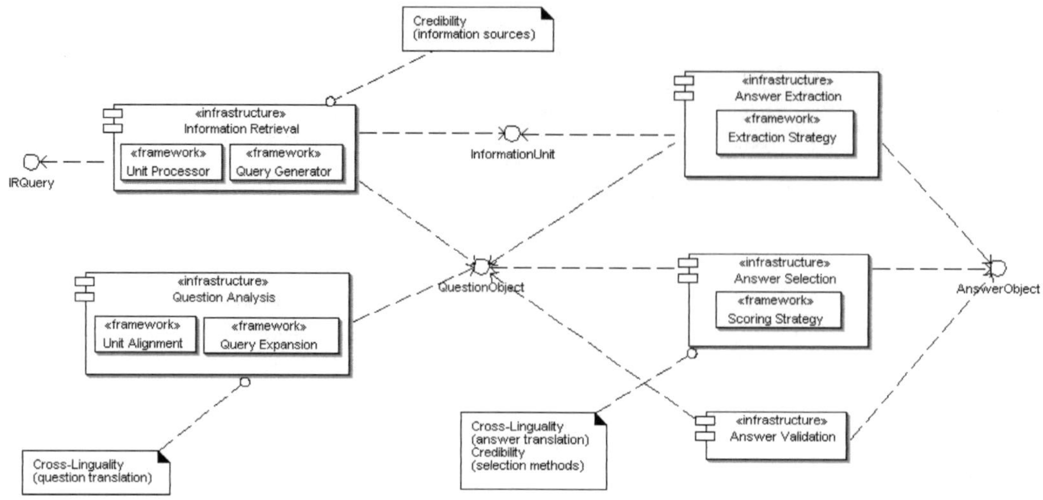

Figure 1: Framework Architecture

Beside the reusability aspect in context of a QA framework, `extensibility` is a further important issue. We have approached it by concentrating on a flexible representation format of the data being passed around in the framework, namely the representation of the `QuestionObject`, the `InformationUnit` and the `AnswerObject`.

2.1 Reusability

"Reusability is the likelihood a segment of structured code can be used again to add new functionalities with slight or no modification". (Wikipedia)

In a cross-language setting of a QA system, which is crossing the language barrier at the user end rather then at the document end, there are two approaches for getting the formalized user information need (`QuestionObject`) to the documents' language: either creating it based on the question translation or analyzing the original question and translating the formalized result. This last approach is convenient when machine readable dictionaries, part-of-speech taggers and other bilingual lexical resources (i.e. WordNets) for both languages are available. For this purpose a `Unit Alignment` Component was designed that produces an alignment of simple (words) and complex (phrases) syntactic units from the source to target language.

`Query Expansion` is another component present among the support structures of our framework. Backed by lexico-semantic resources as EuroWordNet [V98] it can be used for all languages supported by these resource. For a given input word, it can return synonyms, hyponyms and hypernyms according to the following algorithm:

```
if (trgtWord_is_not_ambig)
    return Information;
else if (trgtWord_is_ambig)
{
TRANS:
    1. translate Question
    2. do Unit Alignment
    3. if (transTrgtWord_is_EWN_aligned)
        a. if (alignment_is_not_ambig)
               return Information;
        b. else if (alignment_is_ambig)
               save Alignments;
               goto TRANS;
}

intersection = intersect_saved_alignments();
if (intersection.size == N)        // strict N=1
    return Information_for_intersection;
return NULL;
```

An example for the above algorithm up to the stage 3.a is given in Section 3.1. This represents the ideal case, when our input can be disambiguated using the alignments of a question translation. But more often it is the case of advancing over this stage to 3.b, when the ambiguous EuroWordNet alignments are being saved and a new translation of the question through other online translation services is attempted. The idea behind this expansion method is that lexical diversity of different translations could narrow down the ambiguity of a word to a desired level (N).

To select an initial set of information units relevant to the question, traditional search engines are being used to scale down the search space. Two important aspects in this process are: the level of detail at which the indexation units are chosen and the granularity of the information units (be it document, paragraph, sentence or phrase). Two subcomponents are important at this stage: the `Unit Processor` and the `Query Generator`.

The `Unit Processor` covers the above-mentioned aspects: it takes as input an `InformationUnit` (i.e., a raw text document) and it either reduces it to a set of new units (i.e., sentences), or it annotates the unit at different levels (i.e., named entities, grammatical relations). This way, by chaining different `Unit Processors`, you can both reduce the information unit size and generate new indexing units.

The `Query Generator` relies on an abstract description of the processing method to accordingly generate the `IRQuery` to make use of the advanced indexation units. For example, when named entities were annotated during the `Unit Processor` chaining and used as indexing units, the `Query Generator` will adapt the `IRQuery` so as to search for an additional field (`neType`) that might reflect the expected answer type for the question considered. We consider the `Query Generator` as being the mediator between the question analysis result `QuestionObject` (answer type, constraints) and the search engine serving the retrieval component with information units (documents, sentences). Even more, the `Query Generator` relies on an abstract description of the search engine, too, and can adapt the `IRQuery` according to either a boolean or a ranked search engine.

A `Mention Chain` component in the Answer Extraction task provides an ease of burden for the Selection task by computing answer reference chains. This is very helpful for factoid questions on the Web, and not only, where redundancy of an answer candidate is a good hint for its potential selection and credibility. A mention chain contains all answers sharing a common normalized representation, determined either through the string similarity of the answers only or by additionally employing context entailment measures.

The `Scoring Strategy` component builds on the mathematical graph theory and reduces the answer candidate scoring issue to a shortest path problem on lexical graphs. In most of the cases the answer "suitability" could be scaled down to computing a distance metric for the answer and some information in the question (i.e., keywords, focus). Both a simple textual distance measure and another one based on dependency structures were implemented on these graph structures, with slight variations making use of weight and cost properties for graph edges.

Based on available web search API (i.e., Google, Yahoo) the `Answer Validation` component computes a total frequency count of co-occurrence for pairs of question and answer, assuming that the right answer shares more contexts with the question than any other candidate and that the considered answers are semantic independent and insensitive with respect to the timeline preferred by the search engines.

2.2 Extensibility

"Extensibility is a system design principle where the implementation takes into consideration future growth. ... The central theme is to provide for change while minimizing impact to existing system functions." (Wikipedia)

Extensibility can be approached by two methods during framework design: through software design patterns and through a common extensible data representation format. While we have used some patterns through the development of reusable components like the chaining aspect in the Unit Processor, the normalization function in the Mention Chain and the graph design in the Scoring Strategy, we have concentrated more on an extensible representation format for data being passed around through the framework: the `QuestionObject`, the `InformationUnit` and the `AnswerObject`. For this purpose we have used XML, XML Schema and data binding methods (JAXB) to guarantee component life on an evolving data format. The primary benefit of allowing extensibility in a format is that it enables a format to evolve without requiring central control of the format. A secondary benefit is that it allows the format to stay focused and simple by pushing specialized cases and complex solutions into optionally supported extensions. W3C XML Schema provides two features that promote extensibility in XML vocabularies: the wildcards `xs:any` and `xs:anyAttribute` are used to allow the occurrence of elements and attributes from specified namespaces into a given format, and the `xsi:type` attribute that can be placed on an element in an XML instance document to change its type to a more refined subtype. That is, according to user's need, the data exchanged among the framework's components can be extended, without changing the framework functionality.

3 QA Cross-Cutting Aspects

In a question answering framework there are aspects that does not directly relate to the core concerns, but are needed for a proper design. Moreover, they can hardly be pinned down to a component, as they cross several core components of the system. We are talking about concepts like cross-linguality and credibility – system credibility reflected in answer credibility.

3.1 Cross-Linguality

There are three traditional approaches that count for cross–linguality in context of information management systems:

- translating the queries into the target language,
- translating the document collection into the source language or
- translating the queries and the documents into an intermediate representation (inter–lingua).

Two types of translation services are well known within this context which are based on

- lexical resources (e.g., dictionaries, aligned wordnets), or
- machine translation (e.g., example–based translation).

The only feasible approach when dealing with huge amounts of data, as is the case for question answering systems, is translating the question into the language of the document collection and the related issue of back-translating the answers into the language of the user.

We are using two different methods for responding questions asked in a language different from the one of the answer-bearing documents. Both employ online translation services (Altavista, FreeTranslation, etc.) for crossing the language barrier, but at different processing steps: before and after formalizing the user information need into a `QuestionObject`.

The `before-method` translates the question string in an earlier step, resulting in several automatic translated strings, of which the best one is analyzed by the Question Analysis component and passed on to the Information Retrieval component. This is the strategy we use in an English–German cross-lingual setting. To be more precise: the English source question is translated into several alternative German questions using online MT services. Each German question is then parsed with SMES [NP02], our German parser. The resulting query object is then weighted according to its linguistic well–formedness and its completeness wrt. query information (question type, question focus, answer–type).

The assumption behind this weighting scheme is that "a translated string is of greater utility for subsequent processes than another one, if its linguistic analysis is more complete or appropriate."

The `after-method` translates the formalized result of the Query Analysis Component by using the question translations, a language modeling tool and a word alignment tool for creating a mapping of the formal information need from the source language into the target language. We illustrate this strategy in a German–English setting along two lines (using the following German question as example: `In welchem Jahrzehnt investierten japanische Autohersteller sehr stark?`):

- translations as returned by the on-line MT systems are being ranked according to a language model

```
In which decade did Japanese
automakers invest very
strongly? (0.7)
In which decade did Japanese
car manufacturers invest
very strongly? (0.8)
```

- translations with a satisfactory degree of resemblance to a natural language utterance (i.e. linguistically well-formedness), given by a threshold on the language model ranking, are aligned based on several filters: back-propagation dictionary filter - based on MRD (machine readable dictionaries), PoS filter - based on statistical part-of-speech taggers, and cognates filter - based on string similarity measures (dice coefficient and LCSR (lowest common substring ratio)).

```
In: [in:1]
welchem: [which:0.5]
Jahrzehnt: [decade:1]
investierten: [invest:1]
```

```
japanische: [Japanese:0.5]
Autohersteller:
    [car manufacturers:0.8,
      auto makers:0.1]
sehr: [very:1]
stark: [strongly:0.5]
```

The evaluation gives evidence that both strategies are comparable in results, whereby the last one is slightly better, due to the fact of not being forced to choose a best translation, but working with and combining all the translations available. That is, considering and combining several, possible different, translations of the same question, the chance of detecting a translation error in an earlier phase of the work–flow becomes higher and avoids error propagations through the whole system.

The related issue of back-translating is explored by looking for parallel data to the answer's context or metadata, and extracting translation candidates based on their context and string surface similarity. For example, in a CLEF setting, for a German question having as English answer "Yasser Arafat" we have extracted the time-stamp of the answer's context (19.07.1994), collected all the data with a time-stamp of 07.1994 in the source language, extracted the named entities of type PERSON and then aligned "Jassir Arafat" based on its string surface similarity to the initial answer.

The translations and their alignment to the original question, according to the above-mentioned `after-method`, have also a positive side-effect, namely: some of the aligned words may have several ranked translations. As it is the case of the "Autohersteller", a word might consider the best ranked alignment ("car manufacturers") as its direct translation and the remaining ones as its expanded words. As such, given a reliable alignment method, cross-linguality can prove supportive even for `Query Expansion`. Moreover, another method of usage can confirm the added value of cross-linguality for `Query Expansion`, as described below.

For this task we are using the German and the English wordnets aligned within the EuroWordNet [V98] lexical resource. Our goal is to extend the formalized information need `Question Object` with synonyms for the words that are present in the wordnet.

Considering the ambiguity of words, a WSD module is required as part of the expansion task. For this purpose we are using both the original question and its translations, leveraging the reduction in ambiguity gained through translation. Our devised `pseudo-WSD algorithm` works as following:

1. look up every word from the word-translation alignment (see example above) in the lexical resource;

2. if the word is not ambiguous (which is, for example, the case for `Japanese`) then extend the Question Object with its synonyms (e.g., `[Japanese, Nipponese]`);

3. if the word is ambiguous (e.g., invest) then

(3a) for every possible reading of it, get its aligned German correspondent reading (if it exists) and look up that reading in the German original question , e.g.,

`1351398:` adorn-clothe-invest `(EN)`
`1351223:` invest-vest `(EN)`
`1400771:` empower-endow-endue-gift-indue-invest `(EN)`
`1350325:` induct-invest-seat `(EN)`
`1293271:`

- commit-invest-place-`put` `(EN)`
- anlegen-investieren (DE)

(3b) if an aligned reading is found (e.g., Reading-`1293271`) retain it and add the English synonyms of it to the Question Object, i.e., expand it with:

`commit, place, put`

Following the question expansion task, the Question Object has been enriched with new words that are synonyms of the un–ambiguous English words and by synonyms of those ambiguous words, whose meaning(s) have been found in the original German question. Thus our expanded example has gained several more expanded words as follows:

`{Nipponese,commit,place,put}`

3.2 Answer Credibility

In the ideal case, a Questions Answering System (QAS) will deliver correct answers *and* knows that they are correct, i.e., it can deliver a proof of the correctness of the answers. However, at least for the case of open-domain textual QA applications, this is out of reach with current technology. Thus, current QAS can only deliver answers with certain *trustworthyness*. Since, a receiver of an answer usually assumes, that a QAS tries to identify the best answer possible (at least for cooperative language games), the QAS should assign a credibility measure to each selected answer. The underlying decisions made, can then also be used for explaining, how the answer's credibility was determined.

We view answer credibility as an additional process to answer extraction and selection that determines the quality of identified answer candidates by checking the plausibility of the answer sources and context on basis of *meta* information. For example, useful document and web page information might be:[1]

- The name of the author of this activity;
- Textual fingerprints of authority, e.g., "official web page of US government";
- E-mail address of the contact person for this activity;
- When was this webpage last updated and links were checked (also: is there an regular update);
- The name of the host school or organization;
- The link structure of the document, e.g., link IN/OUT density, links to relevant people, other authorities, clusters / hierarchies of authorities;
- Text structure, e.g., textual coherence or style;

Another important source of meta information relates to ontological knowledge, e.g., the consistency of contextual information with respect to a domain ontology that defines the scope of the answer candidates. By this we mean the following:

- Given an answer candidate A of a question Q (e.g., an instance of a concept in question) determined by a web-based QAS.
- Check the textual context of A concerning the mentioning of other relevant facts/concepts, that can be determined via access to an external (domain) ontology using relevant terms from Q and A.

For example, if the following request is sent to a web-based QAS: *Name IE-systems that are based on statistical methods.* Assume that for this question, the QAS identifies a list of names of IE-systems from textual sources as answer candidates. Assume further, that the QAS has access to an ontology-based meta-store about Language Technology terms, cf. [JU05]. Then, answer credibility checking can use the query terms *IE-system* and *statistical method* for extracting relevant facts from this LT-store, e.g., names of statistical methods, IE experts, IE subtasks or properties of the concept *information extraction*. Next, for each answer candidate, check the textual context of the answer for the mentioning of these terms and their mutual relationship. Then a possible credibility heuristics might decide that the more relevant domain-knowledge can be identified in the context of the answer the higher is the credibility of this answer.

These examples demonstrate that a wide variety of metadata from different levels can be and should be exploited for determining the credibility of answers. Since answer credibility is a new research area, it is still unclear which level of information is best suited for which kind of questions and answers. In order to be able to investigate many possible credibility scenarios, we consider answer credibility as a complex abstract data type or QAS credibility model, **QAS-CM** for short. The QAS-CM allows the definition of different kinds of credibility parameters, which are related to corresponding meta data and are orthogonal to the component-oriented view of the QAS. The values of the parameters might be computed and evaluated by different components, even in parallel. Thus, the credibility of an answer is a complex value determined through composition of component-related credibility values. We are distinguishing two types of metadata:

- **Static metadata**: are available directly through the textual source of an answer candidate and are represented in form of annotations, e.g. HTML/XML tags.
- **Dynamic metadata**: are computed online via the components of the QAS, e.g., linguistic entities, semantic relations, textual entailment, text structure and coherence, topic linkage.

[1] For information on the topic of Web Credibility, cf. http://credibility.stanford.edu/ . This URL links to the Web Credibility Project of the Stanford Persuasive Technology Lab. Although they do not consider credibility under a strict QA perspective as we do, their work and results are a rich source of inspiration.

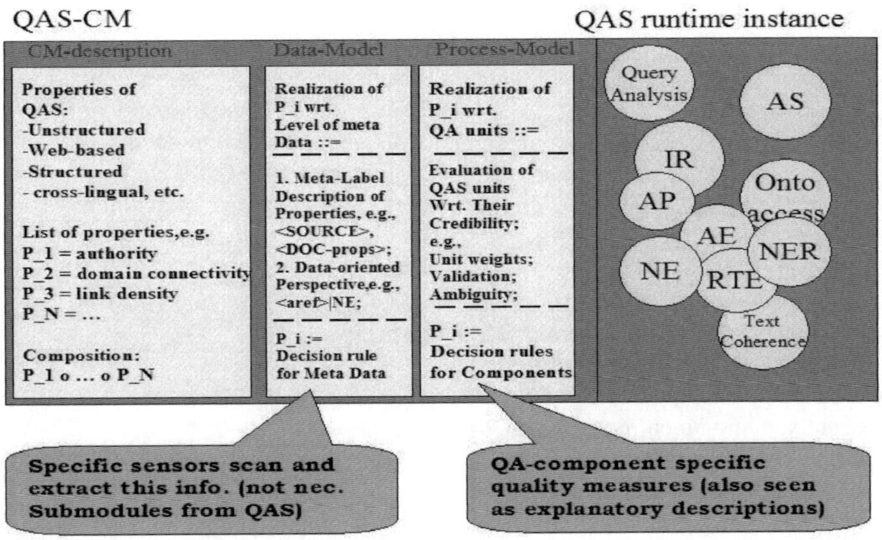

Figure 2. Credibility Model

Following this perspective, we propose the following structure for the QAS-CM (see Figure 2). We distinguish two major subsystems: the QAS-CM itself and the QAS runtime instance. The QAS-CM is further subdivided into three modules:

1. CM-description
2. Data-Model
3. Process-Model

The **CM-description** module defines the credibility properties in a declarative way independently from the specific QAS instance used. It defines the name space of the credibility properties that are to be implemented and the way they are composed. We assume that each individual credibility property returns a real number, i.e., we consider it as a *utility function*, cf. [RN03]. Thus, the composition rules define how a complex value is computed, e.g., by summation or multiplication. The CM-description also contains specification about the actual QAS instance, e.g., the type of document source or natural language to be processed. The CM-description serves as a blueprint for the other two modules, the Data-Model and the Process-Model.

The **Data-Model** implements credibility properties as decision rules over instantiated meta information taking into account either static or dynamic meta data. For example a rule like

```
entails(<SOURCE>,"official
web page of <LOCATION>") →
authority:=αI
```

assigns the weight α_I to the credibility property with name `authority` if the document source of the answer candidate has a tag `<source>` which contains a substring "`official web page <LOCATION>`", where `<LOCATION>` contains a location name which corresponds to one mentioned in the Wh-question. For a question like "Name all German chancellors after World War II.", then an answer with a web page source, that contains something like `<SOURCE> … official web page of Germany … </SOURCE>` will receive a credibility value α_I.

The **Process-Model** is related to the components of the QAS that have been used for the processing of a question/answer pair. We assume that each component can assign a utility measure for its determined output. In doing so, a component should also take into account the size and utility measure of its input and the ambiguity degree of its output etc. For example, assume that the question analysis component (cf. sec. 3) can recognize the syntactic quality of a parse tree of a Wh-question, as being `complete`, `partial` or `null`, cf. [NS05a]. Then a possible decision rule for the Process-Model might be

```
syntactic_quality(<QUESTION>
, COMPLETE) → QueryAna-
lyser:=αI=1
```

in case, the parser of the question analysis component was able to completely parse the Wh-question `<QUESTION>`. In a similar way, the web-validator mentioned in sec. 2.1 can also be integrated as a credibility function into our QAS-CM using the following decision rule:

```
validate(Web, <QUESTION>,
<CurrAnsw>) → WebValua-
tor:=αI
```

Note that in case statistical components are used in QAS, e.g., a stochastic NE-recognizer, then the probabilities of the those components can be used for defining the utility values for the representative decision rules. Furthermore note, that each decision rule of the Process-Model corresponds to a single component. The compositon of several such rules are defined in the CM-description module.

We are currently implementing QAS-CM following the same object-oriented framework as described in sec. 3, which eases integration of the components of the QAS. The data and the process model are implemented as a set of production rules using the RuleML language, cf. http://www.ruleml.org/. Currently, we define the values of α_I manually. This is more easier to implement but more tricky to maintain because of potential mutual interdependencies between individual values. Therefore, in the next development cycle of our QAS-CM, we will use a statistical approach for automatically acquiring optimal parameter settings. Starting point will be a question/answer/document corpus. This corpus can directly be used for training the Data-Model. In the case of the Process-Model, a Bayesian Network will be dynamically trained following ideas from IE-research, cf. [PP03]. Since in this case we also need output from all major QAS components, we are integrating an exhaustive tracing mechanism into our QA framework as a basis for automatically determining initial training material.

4 Results

The presented QA framework has been used both in mono-lingual and cross-lingual scenarios for closed document collections (CLEF collection) and open document collections (World Wide Web). In terms of reusability and extensibility, the framework allowed for up to two weeks of work for building fully functional QA systems for different use scenarios. In terms of time performance for systems build upon the framework, the following figures apply: for systems used to query the Web a response time of up to 20 seconds in mono-lingual settings could be measured; those querying the CLEF document collection in a mono-lingual setting (German only) registered a latency of up to 3 seconds and for a cross-lingual setting of up to 15 seconds. The qualitative performance has been measured only on closed document collection and the best results for 200 questions of the CLEF 2005 evaluation campaign in different use scenarios, according to [NS05b], were as follows:

	Right		Wrong	Inexact
DeDe	87	43.5%	100	13
DeEn	51	25.5%	141	8
EnDe	46	23%	141	12

Reference

[JU05] B. Jörg and H. Uszkoreit. The Ontology-based Architecture of LT World, a Comprehensive Web Information System for a Science and Technology Discipline. Leitbild Informationskompetenz: Positionen - Praxis - Perspektiven im europäischen Wissensmarkt. 27. Online Tagung, 2005.

[NP02] G. Neumann and J. Piskorski. A shallow text processing core engine. Computational Intelligence, 18(3):451–476, 2002.

[NS05a] G. Neumann and S. Sacaleanu. Experiments on robust NL-question interpretation and multi-layered document annotation for a cross-language question/answering system. In Clef 2004, volume 3491. Springer-Verlag LNCS, 2005.

[NS05b] G. Neumann and B. Sacaleanu. DFKI's LT-lab at the CLEF 2005 Multiple Language Question AnsweringTrack. In Working Notes for the CLEF 2005 Workshop, 21-23 September, Vienna, Austria, 2005.

[PP03] L. Peshkin and A. Pfefer. Bayesian Information Extraction Network. In proceedings of IJCAI, 2003.

[RN03] S. Russell and P. Norvig. *Artificial Intelligence: A Modern Approach.* Prentice-Hall, Englewood Cliffs, NJ, 2nd edition, 2003.

[V98] Vossen, P. (eds) 1998 *EuroWordNet: A Multilingual Database with Lexical Semantic Networks*, Kluwer Academic Publishers, Dordrecht.

Evaluation and Improvement of Cross-Lingual Question Answering Strategies

Anne-Laure Ligozat and **Brigitte Grau** and **Isabelle Robba** and **Anne Vilnat**
LIMSI-CNRS
91403 Orsay Cedex, France
firstname.lastname@limsi.fr

Abstract

This article presents a bilingual question answering system, which is able to process questions and documents both in French and in English. Two cross-lingual strategies are described and evaluated. First, we study the contribution of biterms translation, and the influence of the completion of the translation dictionaries. Then, we propose a strategy for transferring the question analysis from one language to the other, and we study its influence on the performance of our system.

1 Introduction

When a question is asked in a certain language on the Web, it can be interesting to look for the answer to the question in documents written in other languages in order to increase the number of documents returned. The CLEF evaluation campaign for cross-language question answering systems addresses this issue by encouraging the development of such systems.

The objective of question answering systems is to return precise answers to natural-language questions, instead of the list of documents usually returned by a search engine. The opening to multilingualism of question answering systems raises issues both for the Information Retrieval and the Information Extraction points of view.

This article presents a cross-language question answering system able to treat questions and documents either in French or in English. Two different strategies for shifting language are evaluated, and several possibilities of evolution are presented.

2 Presentation of our question answering system

Our bilingual question answering system has participated in the CLEF 2005 evaluation campaign [1]. The CLEF QA task aims at evaluating different question answering systems on a given set of questions, and a given corpus of documents, the questions and the documents being either in the same language (except English) or in two differents languages. Last year, our system participated in the French to English task, for which the questions are in French and the documents to search in English.

This system is composed of several modules that are presented Figure 1. The first module analyses the questions, and tries to detect a few of their characteristics, that will enable us to find the answers in the documents. Then the collection is processed thanks to MG search engine [2]. The documents returned are reindexed according to the presence of the question terms, and more precisely to the number and type of these terms ; next, a module recognizes the named entities, and the sentences from the documents are weighted according to the information on the question. Finally, different processes are applied depending on the expected answer type, in order to extract answers from the sentences.

3 Cross-language strategies for question answering systems

Two main approaches are possible to deal with multilingualism in question answering systems :

[1] Multilingual Question Answering task at the Cross Language Evaluation Forum, http ://clef-qa.itc.it/

[2] MG for Managing Gigabytes http ://www.cs.mu.oz.au/mg/

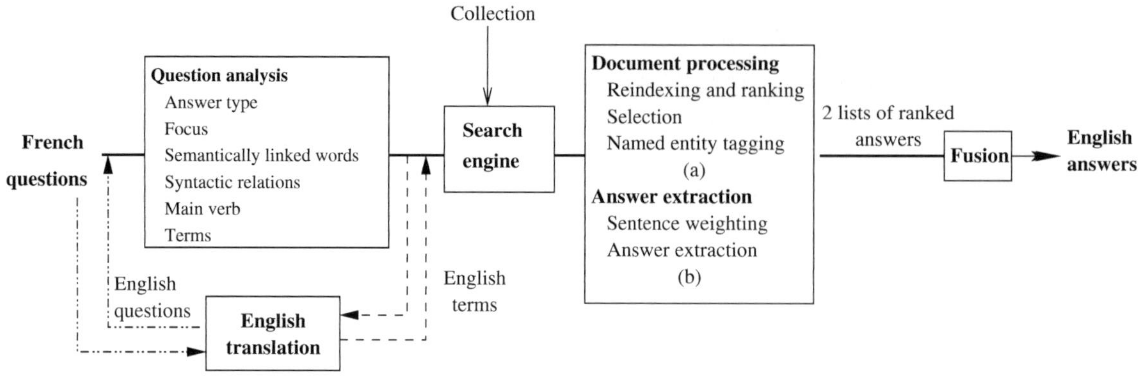

FIG. 1 – Architecture of our cross-language question answering system

question translation and term-by-term translation. These approaches have been implemented and evaluated by many systems in the CLEF evaluations, which gives a wide state-of-the-art of this domain and of the possible cross-language strategies.

The first approach consists in translating the whole question into the target language, and then processing the question analysis in this target language. This approach is the most widely used, and has for example been chosen by the following systems : (Perret, 2004), (Jijkoun et al., 2004), (Neumann and Sacaleanu, 2005), (de Pablo-Sánchez et al., 2005), (Tanev et al., 2005). Among these systems, several have measured the performance loss between their monolingual and their bilingual systems. Thus, the English-French version of (Perret, 2004) has a 11 % performance loss (in terms of absolute loss), dropping from 24.5% to 13.5% of correct answers. The English-Dutch version of (Jijkoun et al., 2004)'s system has an approximative 10% performance loss of correct answers : the percentage of correct answers drops from 45.5% to 35%. As for (de Pablo-Sánchez et al., 2005), they lose 6% of correct answers between their Spanish monolingual system and their English-Spanish bilingual system. (Hartrumpf, 2005) also conducted an experiment by translating the questions from English to German, and reports a drop from about 50% of performance.

For their cross-language system, (Neumann and Sacaleanu, 2004) chose to use several machine translation tools, and to gather the different translations into a "bag of words" that is used to expand queries. Synonyms are also added to the "bag of words" and EuroWordNet [3] is used to disambiguate. They lose quite few correct answers between their German monolingual system and their German-English bilingual system, with which they obtain respectively 25 and 23.5% of correct answers.

Translating the question raises two main problems : syntactically incorrect questions may be produced, and the resolution of translation ambiguities may be wrong. Moreover, the unknown words such as some proper names are not or incorrectly translated. We will describe later several possibilities to deal with these problems, as well as our own solution.

Other systems such as (Sutcliffe et al., 2005) or (Tanev et al., 2004) use a term-by-term translation. In this approach, the question is analyzed in the source language and then the information returned by the question analysis is translated into the target language. (Tanev et al., 2004), who participated in the Bulgarian-English and Italian-English tasks in 2004, translate the question keywords by using bilingual dictionaries and MultiWordNet [4]. In order to limit the noise stemming from the different translations and to have a better cohesion, they validate the translations in two large corpora, AQUAINT and TIPSTER. This system got a score of 22.5% of correct answers in the bilingual task, and 28% in the monolingual task in 2004. (Sutcliffe et al., 2005) combine two translation tools and a dictionary to translate phrases. Eventually, (Laurent et al., 2005) also translate words or idioms, by using English as a pivot language. The performance of this system is of 64% of correct answers for the French monolingual task, and

[3]Multilingual database with wordnets for several European languages, http ://www.illc.uva.nl/EuroWordNet/

[4]Multilingual lexical database in which the Italian WordNet is strictly aligned with Princeton WordNet, http ://multiwordnet.itc.it

39.5% for the English-French bilingual task.

4 Adopted approach

In order to deal with the conversion from French to English in our system, two strategies are applied in parallel. They differ on what is translated to treat the question asked in French. The first subsystem called MUSQAT proceeds to the question analysis in French, and then translates the question terms extracted by this question analysis module, following the - - - arrows in Figure 1. The second sub-system makes use of a machine translation tool (Reverso [5]) to obtain translations of the questions and then our English monolingual system called QALC is applied, following the ..-.. arrows in Figure 1 . These strategies will be detailed later in the article.

If they represent the most common strategies for this kind of task, an original feature of our system is the implementation of both strategies, which enables us to merge the results obtained by following these strategies, in order to improve the global performance of our system.

In Table 1, we present an analysis of the results we obtained for the CLEF evaluation campaign. We evaluate the results obtained at two different points of the question-answering process, i.e. after the sentence selection (point (a) in Figure 1), and after the answer extraction (point (b) in Figure 1). At point (a), we count how many questions (among the global evaluation set of 200 questions) have an appropriate answer in the first five sentences. At point (b), we distinguish the answers the analysis process labels as named entities (NE), from the others, since the corresponding answering processes are different. We also detail how many answers are ranked first, or in the first five ranks, as we take into account the first five answers.

As illustrated in Table 1, the two strategies for dealing with multilingualism give quite different results, which can be explained by each strategy characteristics.

MUSQAT proceeds to the question analysis with French questions correctly expressed, and which analysis is therefore more reliable. Yet, the terms translations are then obtained from every possible translation of each term, and thus without taking account any context ; moreover, they depend on the quality of the dictionaries used, and

		MUSQAT %	Reverso +QALC %
(a) : Sentences with an answer	first 5 ranks	41	46
(b) : Correct NE answers	rank 1	18	14
	first 5 ranks	26	17
(b) : Correct other answers	rank 1	16	13
	first 5 ranks	23	20
(b) : Total (NE + non NE)	rank 1	17	13
	first 5 ranks	24	19
Final result (fusion of both strategies)		19	

TAB. 1 – Performance of our system in CLEF 2005

introduce noise because of the erroneous translations.

In MUSQAT, we do not only translate monoterms (i.e. terms composed of single word) : the biterms (composed of two words) of the French questions are also extracted by the question analysis. Every sequence of two terms which are tagged as *adjective/common noun* or *proper noun/proper noun*... constitutes a biterm. Each word of the biterm is translated, and then the existence of the corresponding biterm built in English is checked in the corpus. The biterms thus obtained are then used by the further modules of the system. Taking biterms into account is useful since they provide a minimal context to the words forming them, as well for the translation as for the re-indexing and re-ranking of the documents (see Figure 1), as explained in (Ferret et al., 2002). Moreover, the presence of the biterm translations in the corpus is a kind of validation of the monoterms translations.

As for translating the question, which is implemented by Reverso+QALC, it presents the advantage of giving a unique translation of the question terms, which is quite reliable. But the grammaticality or realism of the question are not assured, and thus the question analysis, based on regular expression patterns, can be disturbed.

In this work, we tried to evaluate each strategy

[5] http ://www.reverso.net/

and to bypass their drawbacks : on the one hand (Section 5), by examining how the biterm translation in MUSQAT could be more reliable, and on the other hand (Section 6) by improving the question analysis, by relying on the French questions, for QALC.

5 Biterm translation

The translation of terms and biterms present in the question is achieved using two dictionaries. The first of them, which was used last year for our participation to CLEF is Magic-Dic [6]. It is a dictionary under GPL licence, which was retained for its capacity to evolve. Indeed users can submit new translations which are controlled before being integrated. Yet, it is quite incomplete. This year we used FreeDict as well (FreeDict is also under GPL licence), to fill in the gaps of Magic-Dic. FreeDict added 424 translations to the 690 terms already obtained. By mixing both sets of translations we obtained 463 additional biterms, making a total of 777 biterms.

Nevertheless, whatever the quality and the size of the dictionaries are, the problem of biterm translation remains the same : since biterms are not in the dictionaries, the only way for us to get their translation is to combine all the different term translations. The main drawback of this approach is the generated noise, for none of the terms constituting the biterm is disambiguated. For example, three different translations are found for the biterm *Conseil de défense* : *defense council*, *defense advice* and *defense counsel* ; but only the first of those should be finally retained by our system.

To reduce this noise, an interesting possibility is to validate the obtained biterms by searching them or their variants in the complete collection of documents. (Grefenstette, 1999) reports a quite similar experiment in the context of a machine translation task : he uses the Web in order to order the possible translations of noun phrases, and in particular noun biterms. Fastr (Jacquemin, 1996) is a parser which takes as input a corpus and a list of terms (multi or monoterms) and outputs the indexed corpus in which terms and their variants are recognized. Hence, Fastr is quite adequate for biterms validation : it tags all the biterms present in the collection, whether in their original form or in a variant that can be semantic or syntactic.

In order to validate the biterms, the complete collection of the CLEF campaign (500 Mbyte) was first tagged using the TreeTagger, then Fastr was applied. The results are presented Table 2 : 39.5% of the 777 biterms were found in the collection, in a total of 63,404 occurrences. Thus there is an average of 206 occurrences for each biterm. If we do not take into account the biterm which is the most represented (*last year* with 30,981 occurrences), this average falls to 105. The 52 biterms which are found in their original form only are most of the time names of persons. Lastly, biterms that are never found in their original form, are often constituted of one term badly translated, for example the biterm *oil importation* is not present in the collection but its variant *import of oil* is found 28 times. Then, it may be interesting to replace these biterms by the most represented of their variants.

Whenever a biterm is thus validated (found in the collection beyond a chosen threshold), the translation of its terms is itself validated, other translations being discarded. Thus, biterm validation enables us to validate monoterm translations. Then, the following step will be to evaluate how this new set of terms and biterms improves the results of MUSQAT.

After CLEF 2005 evaluation, we had at our disposal the set of questions in their English original version (this set was provided by the organizers). We had also the English translation (far less correct) provided by the automatic translator Reverso.

As we can see it Table 3, for each set of questions the number of terms and biterms is nearly the same. In the set of translations given by Reverso, we manually examined how many biterms were false and found that here again the figures were close to those of the original version. There are two main reasons for which a biterm may be false :

- in two thirds of cases, the association itself is false : the two terms should not have been associated ; it is the case for example of *many country* from the question *How many countries joined the international coalition to restore the democratic government in Haiti ?* [7]
- in one third of cases, one of the terms is not translated or translated with an erroneous term, like *movement zapatiste* coming from the question *What carry the courtiers of the movement zapatiste in Mexico ?* [8]

[6] http ://magic-dic.homeunix.net

[7] This sentence is an example of very good translation given by Reverso

[8] This sentence is an example of bad translation given by

Total Number of biterms	777
Number of biterms found in the collection	307 - 39.5%
Number of biterms found in their original form only	52 - 17%
Number of biterms found with semantic variations only	150 - 54%

TAB. 2 – Magic-Dic and FreeDict biterms validated by Fastr

	Questions in French	Questions translated in English by Reverso	Questions in English (original version)
Terms	1180	1122	1163
Biterms	272	204	261
False Biterms	33	38	27
Common Biterms	-	106	

TAB. 3 – Biterms in the different sets of questions

However, we calculated that among the 204 biterms given by Reverso, 106 are also present in the original set of questions in English. Among the 98 remaining biterms, 38 are false (for the reasons given above). Then, there are 60 biterms which are neither erroneous nor present in the original version. Some of them contain a term which has been translated using a different word, but that is nevertheless correct ; yet, most of these 60 biterms have a different syntax from those constructed from the original version, which is due to the syntax of the questions translated by Reverso.

This leads us to conclude that even if Reverso produces syntactically erroneous questions, the vocabulary it chooses is most of the time adequate. Yet, it is still interesting to use also the biterms constructed from the dictionaries since they are much more numerous and provide variants of the biterms returned by Reverso.

6 Multilingual question analysis

We have developed for the evaluations a question analysis in both languages. It is based on the morpho-syntactic tagging and the syntactic analysis of the questions. Then different elements are detected from both analyses : recognition of the expected answer type, of the question category, of the temporal context...

There are of course lexicons and patterns which are specific to each language, but the core of the module is independent from the language. This module was evaluated on corpora of similar questions in French and in English, and its results on both languages are quite close (around 90% of recall and precision for the expected answer type for example ; for more details, see (Ligozat et al., 2006)).

As presented above, our system relies on two distinct strategies to answer to a cross-language question :

- Either the question is analyzed in the original language, and next translated term-by-term. The question analysis is then more reliable since it processes a grammatically correct question ; yet, the translation of terms has no context to rely on.
- Or the question is first translated into the target language before being analyzed. Although this strategy improves the translation, its main inconvenient is that each translation error has strong consequences on the question analysis. We will now try to evaluate to which extent the translation errors actually influence our question analysis and to find solutions to avoid minimize this influence in the Reverso+QALC system.

An error in the question translation can lead to wrong terms or an incorrect English construction. Thus, the translation of the question "Combien y a-t-il d'habitants en France ?" ("How many inhabitants are there in France ?") is "How much is there of inhabitants in France ?".

In order to evaluate our second strategy, Reverso+QALC, using question translation and then a monolingual system, it is interesting to estimate

Reverso, which should have produced *What do supporters of the Zapatistas in Mexico wear ?*

the influence of a such a coarse translation on the results of our system.

In order to avoid these translating problems, it is possible to adapt either the input or the output of the translating module. (Ahn et al., 2004) present an example of a system processing pre- and post-corrections thanks to surface reformulation rules. However, this type of correction is highly dependent on the kind of questions to process, as well as on the errors of the translation tool that is used.

We suggest to use another kind of processing, which makes the most of the cross-lingual character of the task, in order to improve the analysis of the translated questions and to take into account the possibilities of errors in these questions.

Our present system already takes into account some of the most frequent translation errors, by allowing the question analysis module to loosen some of its rules in case the question be translated. Thus, a definition question such as "Qu'est-ce que l'UNITA ?", translated "What UNITA ?" by our translating tool, instead of "What is the UNITA ?", will nevertheless be correctly analyzed by our rules : indeed, the pattern *WhatGN* will be considered as corresponding to a definition question, while on a non-translated question, only the pattern *WhatBeGN* will be allowed.

In order to try and improve our processing of approximations in the translated questions, the solution we suggest here consists in making the question analysis in both the source and the target languages, and in reporting the information (or at least part of it) returned by the source analysis into the target analysis. This is possible first because our system treats both the languages in a parallel way, and second, some of the information returned by the question analysis module use the same terms in English and in French, like for example the question category or the expected Named Entity type.

More precisely, we propose, in the task with French questions and English documents, to analyse the French questions, and their English translations, and then to report the question category and the expected answer type of the French questions into the English question analysis. The information found in the source language should be more reliable since obtained on a real question.

For example, for the question "Combien de communautés Di Mambro a-t-il crée ?" ("How many communities has Di Mambro created ?"), Reverso's translation is "How many Di Mambro communities has he create ?" which prevents the question analysis module to analyze it correctly. The French analysis is thus used, which provides the question category *combien* (*how many*) and the expected named entity type *NUMBER*. This information is reported in the English analysis file.

These characteristics of the question are used at two different steps of the question answering process : when selecting the candidate sentences and when extracting the answers. Improving their reliability should then enable us to increase the number of correct answers after these two steps.

In order to test this strategy, we conducted an experiment based on the CLEF 2005 FR-EN task, and the 200 corresponding French questions. We launched the question answering system on three question files :

- The first question file (here called English file) contained the original English questions (provided by the CLEF organizers). This file will be considered as a test file, since the results of our system on this file represent those that would be reached without translation errors.
- The second file (called Translated file) contained the translated questions analysis.
- The last file (called Improved file) contained the same analysis, but for which the question category and the expected answer type were replaced by those of the French analysis.

Then we searched for the number of correct answers for each input question file after the sentence selection and after the answer extraction. The results obtained by our system on each file are presented on Figure 2, Figure 3 and Figure 4. These figures present the number of questions expecting a named entity answer, expecting another kind of answer, and the total number of questions, as well as the results of our system on each type of question : the number of correct questions are given at the first five ranks, and at the first rank, first for the sentences ("long answers") and then for the short answers.

These results show that the information transfer from the source language to the target language significantly improves the system's results ; the number of correct answers increases in every case. It increases from 34 on the translated questions file to 36 on the improved file, and from 52

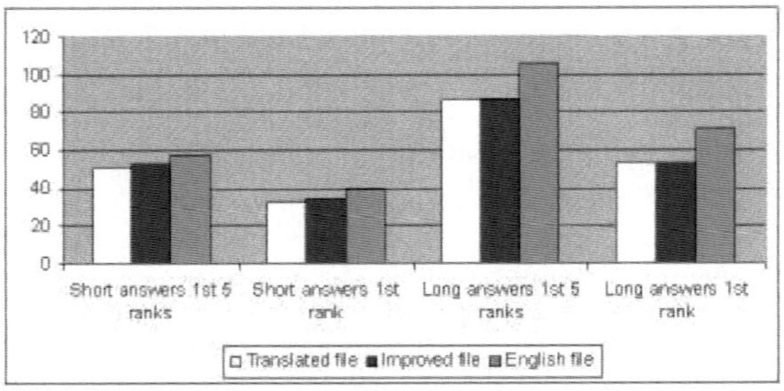

FIG. 2 – QALC's results (i.e. number of correct answers) on the 200 questions

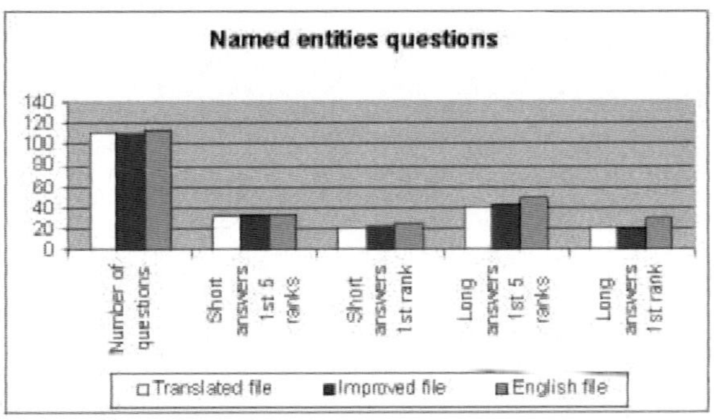

FIG. 3 – Results on the named entities questions

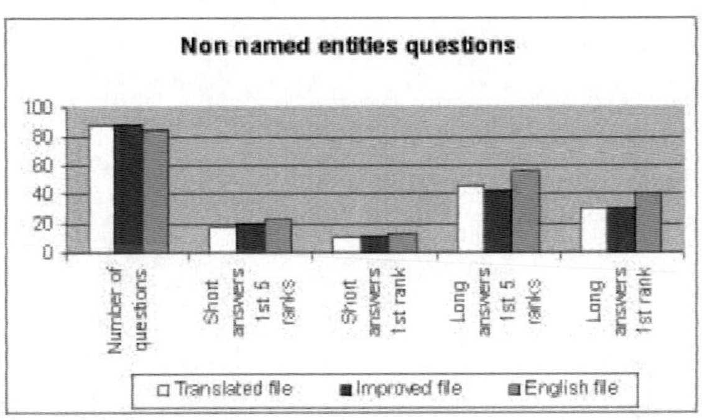

FIG. 4 – Results on the non named entities questions

to 55 for the first 5 ranks. These results are closer to those of the monolingual system, which returns 41 correct answers at the first rank, and 59 on the first 5 ranks.

It is interesting to see that the difference between the monolingual and the bilingual systems is less noticeable after the sentence selection step than after the answer extraction step, which tends to prove that the last step of our process is more sensitive to translation errors. Moreover, this experiment shows that this step can be improved thanks to an information transfer between the source and the target languages. In order to extend this strategy, we could also match each French question term to its English equivalent, in order to translate all the information given by the French analysis into English. Thus, the question analysis errors would be minimized.

7 Conclusion

The originality of our cross-language question answering system is to use in parallel the two most widely used strategies for shifting language, which enables us to benefit from the advantages of each strategy. Yet, each method presents drawbacks, that we tried to evaluate in this article, and to bypass.

For the term-by-term translation, we make the most of the question biterms in order to restrict the possible translation ambiguities. By validating the biterms in the document collection, we have improved the quality of both the biterms and the monoterms translations. We hope this improvement will lead to a better selection of the candidate sentences from the documents.

For the question translation, we use the information deduced from the source language to avoid the problems coming from a bad or approximative translation. This strategy enables us to solve some of the problems coming from non-grammatical translations ; matching each term of the French question with its English equivalent would enable us to transfer all the information of the French analysis. But the disambiguation errors of the translation remain.

References

Kisuh Ahn, Beatrix Alex, Johan Bos, Tiphaine Delmas, Jochen L. Leidner, and Matthew B. Smillie. 2004. Cross-lingual question answering with QED.

In *Working Notes, CLEF Cross-Language Evaluation Forum*, pages 335–342, Bath, UK.

César de Pablo-Sánchez, Ana González-Ledesma, José Luis Martínez-Fernández, José Maria Guirao, Paloma Martinez, and Antonio Moreno. 2005. MIRACLE's 2005 approach to cross-lingual question answering. In *Working Notes, CLEF Cross-Language Evaluation Forum*, Vienna, Austria.

Olivier Ferret, Brigitte Grau, Martine Hurault-Plantet, Gabriel Illouz, Christian Jacquemin, Laura Monceaux, Isabelle Robba, and Anne Vilnat. 2002. How NLP can improve question answering. *Knowledge Organization*, 29(3-4).

Gregory Grefenstette. 1999. The world wide web as a resource for example-based machine translation tasks. In *ASLIB Conference on Translating and the Computer*, volume 21, London, UK.

Sven Hartrumpf. 2005. University of Hagen at QA@CLEF 2005 : Extending knowledge and deepening linguistic processing for question answering. In *Working Notes, CLEF Cross-Language Evaluation Forum*, Vienna, Austria.

Christian Jacquemin. 1996. A symbolic and surgical acquisition of terms through variation. *Connectionist, Statistical and Symbolic Approaches to Learning for Natural Language Processing*, pages 425–438.

Valentin Jijkoun, Gilad Mishne, Maarten de Rijke, Stefan Schlobach, David Ahn, and Karin Muller. 2004. The University of Amsterdam at QA@CLEF2004. In *Working Notes, CLEF Cross-Language Evaluation Forum*, pages 321–325, Bath, UK.

Dominique Laurent, Patrick Séguéla, and Sophie Nègre. 2005. Cross lingual question answering using QRISTAL for CLEF 2005. In *Working Notes, CLEF Cross-Language Evaluation Forum*, Vienna, Austria.

Anne-Laure Ligozat, Brigitte Grau, Isabelle Robba, and Anne Vilnat. 2006. L'extraction des réponses dans un système de question-réponse. In *Traitement Automatique des Langues Naturelles (TALN 2006)*, Leuven, Belgium.

Günter Neumann and Bogdan Sacaleanu. 2004. Experiments on robust NL question interpretation and multi-layered doument annotation for a cross-language question / answering system. In *Working Notes, CLEF Cross-Language Evaluation Forum*, pages 311–320, Bath, UK.

Günter Neumann and Bogdan Sacaleanu. 2005. DFKI's LT-lab at the CLEF 2005 multiple language question answering track. In *Working Notes, CLEF Cross-Language Evaluation Forum*, Vienna, Austria.

Laura Perret. 2004. Question answering system for the French language. In *Working Notes, CLEF Cross-Language Evaluation Forum*, pages 295–305, Bath, UK.

Richard F.E. Sutcliffe, Michael Mulcahy, Igal Gabbay, Aoife O'Gorman, Kieran White, and Darina Slattery. 2005. Cross-language French-English question answering using the DLT system at CLEF 2005. In *Working Notes, CLEF Cross-Language Evaluation Forum*, Vienna, Austria.

Hristo Tanev, Matteo Negri, Bernardo Magnini, and Milen Kouylekov. 2004. The DIOGENE question answering system at CLEF-2004. In *Working Notes, CLEF Cross-Language Evaluation Forum*, pages 325–333, Bath UK.

Hristo Tanev, Milen Kouylekov, Bernardo Magnini, Matteo Negri, and Kiril Simov. 2005. Exploiting linguistic indices and syntactic structures for multilingual question answering : ITC-irst at CLEF 2005. In *Working Notes, CLEF Cross-Language Evaluation Forum*, Vienna, Austria.

Keyword Translation Accuracy and Cross-Lingual Question Answering in Chinese and Japanese

Teruko Mitamura
Carnegie Mellon University
Pittsburgh, PA USA
teruko@cs.cmu.edu

Mengqiu Wang
Carnegie Mellon University
Pittsburgh, PA USA
mengqiu@cs.cmu.edu

Hideki Shima
Carnegie Mellon University
Pittsburgh, PA USA
hideki@cs.cmu.edu

Frank Lin
Carnegie Mellon University
Pittsburgh, PA USA
frank+@cs.cmu.edu

Abstract

In this paper, we describe the extension of an existing monolingual QA system for English-to-Chinese and English-to-Japanese cross-lingual question answering (CLQA). We also attempt to characterize the influence of translation on CLQA performance through experimental evaluation and analysis. The paper also describes some language-specific issues for keyword translation in CLQA.

1 Introduction

The JAVELIN system is a modular, extensible architecture for building question-answering (QA) systems (Nyberg, et al., 2005). Since the JAVELIN architecture is language-independent, we extended the original English version of JAVELIN for cross-language question answering (CLQA) in Chinese and Japanese. The same overall architecture was used for both systems, allowing us to compare the performance of the two systems. In this paper, we describe how we extended the monolingual system for CLQA (see Section 3). Keyword translation is a crucial element of the system; we describe our translation module in Section 3.2. In Section 4, we evaluate the end-to-end CLQA systems using three different translation methods. Language-specific translation issues are discussed in Section 5.

2 Javelin Architecture

The JAVELIN system is composed of four main modules: the Question Analyzer (QA), Retrieval Strategist (RS), Information eXtractor (IX) and Answer Generator (AG). Inputs to the system are processed by these modules in the order listed above. The QA module is responsible for parsing the input question, assigning the appropriate answer type to the question, and producing a set of keywords. The RS module is responsible for finding documents containing answers to the question, using keywords produced by the QA module. The IX module finds and extracts answers from the documents based on the answer type, and then produces a ranked list of answer candidates. The AG module normalizes and clusters the answer candidates to rerank and generate a final ranked list. The overall monolingual architecture is shown in Figure 1.

3 Extension for Cross-Lingual QA

Because of JAVELIN's modular design, significant changes to the monolingual architecture were not required. We customized the system in order to handle Unicode characters and "plug in" cross-lingual components and resources.

For the Question Analyzer, we created the Keyword Translator, a sub-module for translating keywords. The Retrieval Strategist was adapted to search in multilingual corpora. The Information Extractors use language-independent extraction algorithms. The Answer Generator uses language-specific sub-modules for normalization, and a language-independent algorithm for answer ranking. The overall cross-lingual architecture is shown in Figure 2. The rest of this section explains the details of each module.

3.1 Question Analyzer

The Question Analyzer (QA) is responsible for extracting information from the input question in order to formulate a representation of the

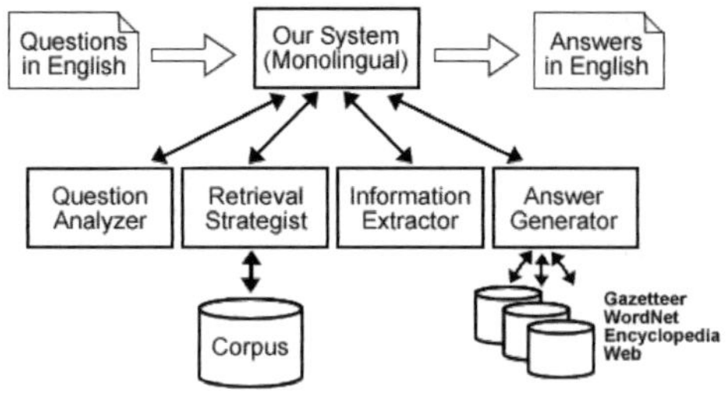

Figure1: Javelin Monolingual Architecture

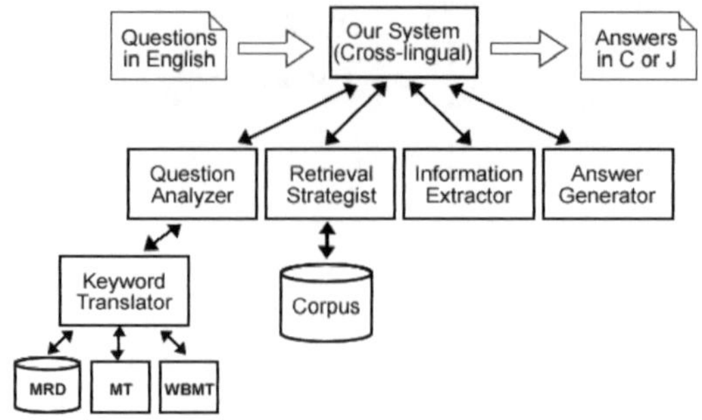

Figure2: Javelin Architecture with Cross-Lingual Extension

information required to answer the question. Input questions are processed using the RASP parser (Korhonen and Briscoe, 2004), and the module output contains three main components: a) selected keywords; b) the answer type (e.g. numeric-expression, person-name, location); and c) the answer subtype (e.g. author, river, city). The selected keywords are words or phrases which are expected to appear in documents with correct answers. In order to reduce noise in the document retrieval phase, we use stop-word lists to eliminate high-frequency terms; for example, the term "old" is not included as a keyword for "how-old" questions.

We extended the QA module with a keyword translation sub-module, so that translated keywords can be used to retrieve documents from multilingual corpora. This straightforward approach has been used by many other CLQA systems. An alternative approach is to first translate the whole question sentence from English to the target language, and then analyze the translated question. Our reasons for favoring keyword translation are two-fold. First, to translate the question to the target language and analyze it, we would have to replace the English NLP components in the Question Analyzer with their counterparts for the target language. In contrast, keyword translation decouples the question analysis from the translation, and requires no language specific resources during question analysis. The second reason is that machine translation is not perfect, and therefore the resulting translation(s) for the question may be incomplete or ungrammatical, thus adding to the complexity of the analysis task. One could argue that when translating the full sentence instead of just the keywords, we can better utilize state-of-art machine translation techniques because more context information is available. But for our application, an accurate translation of functional words (such as prepositions or conjunctions) is less important. We focus more on words that carry more content information, such as verbs and nouns. We will present more detail on the use of contextual information for disambiguation in the next section. In some recent work (Kwok, 2005, Mori and Kawagishi, 2005), researchers have combined these two approaches, but to date no studies have compared their effectiveness.

3.2 Translation Module

The Translation Module (TM) is used by the QA module to translate keywords into the language of the target corpus. Instead of combining multiple translation candidates with a disjunctive query operator (Isozaki et al., 2005), the TM selects the best combination of translated keywords from several sources: Machine Readable Dictionaries (MRDs), Machine Translation systems (MTs) and Web-mining-Based Keyword Translators (WBMTs) (Nagata et al., 2001, Li et al., 2003). For translation from English to Japanese, we used two MRDs, eight MTs and one WBMT. If none of them return a translation, the word is transliterated into kana for Japanese (for details on transliteration, see Section 5.2). For translation from English to Chinese, we used one MRD, three MTs and one WBMT. After gathering all possible translations for every keyword, the TM uses a noisy channel model to select the best combination of translated keywords. The TM estimates model statistics using the World Wide Web. Details of the translation selection method are described in the rest of this subsection.

The Noisy Channel Model: In the noisy channel model, an undistorted signal passes through a noisy channel and becomes distorted. Given the distorted signal, we are to find the original, undistorted signal. IBM applied the noisy channel model idea to translation of sentences from aligned parallel corpora, where the source language sentence is the distorted signal, and the target language sentence is the original signal (Brown et al., 1990). We adopt this model for disambiguating keyword translation, with the source language keyword terms as the distorted signal and the target language terms as the original signal. The TM's job is to find the target language terms given the source language terms, by finding the probability of the target language terms given the source language terms $P(T|S)$.

Using Bayes' Rule, we can break the equation down to several components:

$$P(T \mid S) = \frac{P(T) \cdot P(S \mid T)}{P(S)}$$

Because we are comparing probabilities of different translations of the same source keyword terms, we can simplify the problem to be:

$$P(T \mid S) = P(T) \cdot P(S \mid T)$$

We can now reduce the equation to two components. $P(T)$ is the language model and $P(S|T)$ is the translation model. If we assume independence among the translations of individual terms, we can represent the translation probability of a keyword by the product of the probabilities of the individual term translations:

$$P(S \mid T) = \prod_i P(s_i \mid t_i)$$

Estimating Probabilities using the World Wide Web: For estimating the probabilities of the translation model and the language model, we chose to gather statistics from the World Wide Web. There are three advantages in utilizing the web for gathering translation statistics: 1) it contains documents written in many different languages, 2) it has high coverage of virtually all types of words and phrases, and 3) it is constantly updated. However, we also note that the web contains a lot of noisy data, and building up web statistics is time-consuming unless one has direct access to a web search index.

Estimating Translation Model Probabilities: We make an assumption that terms that are translations of each other co-occur more often in mixed-language web pages than terms that are not translations of each other. This assumption is analogous to Turney's work on the co-occurrence of synonyms (Turney, 2001). We then define the translation probability of each keyword translation as:

$$P(s_i \mid t_{i,j}) = \frac{\log(co(s_i, t_{i,j}))}{\sum_j \log(co(s_i, t_{i,j}))}$$

Where s_i is the i-th term in the source language and $t_{i,j}$ is the j-th translation candidate for s_i. Let hits be a number of web pages retrieved from a certain search engine. $co(s_i, t_{i,j})$ is the hits given a query s_i and $t_{i,j}$., where *log* is applied to adjust the count so that translation probabilities can still be comparable at higher counts.

Estimating Language Model Probabilities: In estimating the language model, we simply obtain hits given a conjunction of all the candidate terms in the target language, and divide that count by the sum of the occurrences of the individual terms:

$$P(T) = \frac{co(t_1, t_2, \ldots t_n)}{\sum_i o(t_i)}$$

The final score of a translation candidate for a query is the product of the translation model score $P(S|T)$ and the language model score $P(T)$.

Smoothing and Pruning: As with most statistical calculations in language technologies, there is a data sparseness problem when calculating the language model score. Also, because statistics are gathered real-time by accessing a remote search engine via internet, it can take a long time to process a single query when there is a large number of translation candidates. We describe methods for smoothing the language model and pruning the set of translation candidates below.

The data sparseness problem occurs when there are many terms in the query, and the terms are relatively rare keywords. When calculating the language model score, it is possible that none of the translation candidates appear on any web page. To address this issue, we propose a "moving-window smoothing" algorithm:

- When the target keyword co-occurrence count with n keywords is below a set threshold for all of the translation candidates, we use a moving window of size n-1 that "moves" through the keywords in sequence, splitting the set of keywords into two sets, each with n-1 keywords.

- If the co-occurrence count of all of these sets of keywords is above the threshold, return the product of the language model score of these two sets as the language model score.

- If not, decrease the window and repeat until either all of the split sets are above the threshold or $n = 1$.

The moving window smoothing technique gradually relaxes the search constraint without losing the "connectivity" of keywords (there is always overlap in the split parts) before finally backing off to just the individual keywords. However, there are two issues worth noting with this approach:

1. "Moving-window smoothing" assumes that keywords that are next to each other are also more semantically related, which may not always be the case.

2. "Moving-window smoothing" tends to give the keywords near the middle of the question more weight, which may not be desirable.

A better smoothing technique may be used with trying all possible "splits" at each stage, but this would greatly increase the time cost. Therefore, we chose the moving-window smoothing as a trade-off between a more robust smoothing technique that tries all possible split combinations and no smoothing at all.

The set of possible translation candidates is produced by creating all possible combinations of the translations of individual keywords. For a question with n keywords and an average of m possible translations per keyword, the number of possible combinations is m^n. This quickly becomes intractable as we have to access a search engine at least m^n times just for the language model score. Therefore, pruning is needed to cut down the number of translation candidates. We prune possible translation candidates twice during each run, using early and late pruning:

1. Early Pruning: We prune possible translations of the individual keywords before combining them to make all possible translations of a query. We use a very simple pruning heuristic based on target word frequency using a word frequency list. Very rare translations produced by a resource are not considered.

2. Late Pruning: We prune possible translation candidates of the entire set of keywords after calculating translation probabilities. Since the calculation of the translation probabilities requires little access to the web, we can calculate only the language model score for the top N candidates with the highest translation score and prune the rest.

An Example of English to Chinese Keyword Translation Selection: Suppose we translate the following question from English to Chinese.

"What if Bush leaves Iraq?"

Three keywords are extracted: "Bush", "leaves", and "Iraq." Using two MT systems and an MRD, we obtain the following translations:

	i=1	i=2	i=3
Source	Bush	leaves	Iraq
Target j=1	灌木	离去	伊拉克
Target j=2	布什	叶子	

Table 1. E-C Keyword Translation

"Bush" and *"leaves"* both have two translations because they are ambiguous keywords, while *"Iraq"* is unambiguous. Translation (1,1) means *bush* as in a *shrub*, and translation (1,2) refers to the person named *Bush*. Translation (2,1) is the verb *"to go away"*, and translation (2,2) is the noun for *leaf*. Note that we would like translation (1,2) and translation (2,1) because they match the sense of the word intended by the user. Now we can create all possible combinations of the keywords in the target language:

"灌木 离去 伊拉克"
"灌木 叶子 伊拉克"
"布什 离去 伊拉克"
"布什 叶子 伊拉克"

Query	"Bush" "灌木"	"Bush" "布什"	"leaves" "离去"	"leaves" "叶子"	"Iraq" "伊拉克"
hits	3790	41100	5780	7240	24500

Table 2. Translation Pair Page Counts

Candidate	Translation Score
"灌木 离去 伊拉克"	0.215615
"灌木 叶子 伊拉克"	0.221219
"布什 离去 伊拉克"	0.277970
"布什 叶子 伊拉克"	0.285195

Table 3. Translation Scores

By calculating hits, we obtain the statistics and the translation scores shown in Table 2 and 3. Now we can proceed to use the search engine to obtain language model statistics, which we use to obtain the language model. Then, together with the translation model score, we calculate the overall score[1].

Query	灌木	布什	离去	叶子	伊拉克
hits	428K	459K	1490K	1100K	9590K

Table 4. Individual Term Page Counts

Query	hits
"灌木 离去 伊拉克"	1200
"灌木 叶子 伊拉克"	455
"布什 离去 伊拉克"	17300
"布什 叶子 伊拉克"	2410

Table 5. Target Language Query Page Counts

Cand	Translation	Language	Overall
灌木 离去 伊拉克	2.1562E-1	1.0428E-4	2.2483E-5
灌木 叶子 伊拉克	2.2122E-1	4.0925E-5	9.0533E-6
布什 离去 伊拉克	2.7797E-1	1.4993E-3	4.1675E-4
布什 叶子 伊拉克	2.8520E-1	2.1616E-4	6.1649E-5

Table 6. Translation Score, Language Model Score, and Overall Score

As shown in Table 6, we select the most probable combination of translated keywords with the highest overall score (the third candidate), which is the correct translation of the English keywords.

3.3 Retrieval Strategies

The Retrieval Strategist (RS) module retrieves documents from a corpus in response to a query. For document retrieval, the RS uses the Lemur 3.0 toolkit (Ogilvie and Callan, 2001). Lemur supports structured queries using operators such as Boolean AND, Synonym, Ordered/Un-Ordered Window and NOT. An example of a structured query is shown below:

```
#BAND( #OD4(邪馬台国 王朝)
       女王
       #SYN(*organization *person) )
```

In formulating a structured query, the RS uses an incremental relaxation technique, starting from an initial query that is highly constrained; the algorithm searches for all the keywords and data types in close proximity to each other. The priority is based on a function of the likely answer type, keyword type (word, proper name, or phrase) and the inverse document frequency of each keyword. The query is gradually relaxed until the desired number of relevant documents is retrieved.

3.4 Information Extraction

In the JAVELIN system, the Information Extractor (IX) is not a single module that uses one extraction algorithm; rather, it is an abstract interface which allows different information extractor implementations to be plugged into JAVELIN. These different extractors can be used to produce different results for comparison, or the results of running them all in parallel can be merged. Here we will describe just one of the extractors, the one which is currently the best algorithm in our CLQA experiment: the Light IX.

The Light IX module uses simple, distance-based algorithms to find a named entity that matches the expected answer type and is "closest" to all the keywords according to some distance measure. The algorithm considers as answer candidates only those terms that are tagged as named entities which match the desired answer type. The score for an answer candidate a is calculated as follows:

$$Score(a) = \alpha \cdot OccScore(a) + \beta \cdot DistScore(a)$$

where $\alpha + \beta = 1$, *OccScore* is the occurrence score and *DistScore* is the distance score. Both *OccScore* and *DistScore* return a number between zero and one, and likewise *Score* returns a number between zero and one. Usually, α is much smaller than β. The occurrence score formula is:

$$OccScore(a) = \frac{\sum_{i=1}^{n} Exist(k_i)}{n}$$

where a is the answer candidate and k_i is the i-th keyword, and n is the number of keywords. *Exist* returns 1 if the i-th keyword exists in the document, and 0 otherwise. The distance score for

[1] For simplicity, we don't apply smoothing and pruning.

each answer candidate is calculated according to the following formula:

$$DistScore(a) = \frac{\sum_{i=1}^{n} \frac{1}{Dist(a,k_i)}}{n}$$

This formula produces a score between zero and one. If the *i*-th keyword does not exist in a document, the equation inside the summation will return zero. If the *i*-th keyword appears more than once in the document, the one closest to the answer candidate is considered. An additional restriction is that the answer candidate cannot be one of the keywords. The Dist function is the distance measure, which has two definitions:

1. $Dist(a,b) = TokensApart(a,b)$
2. $Dist(a,b) = \log(TokensApart(a,b))$

The first definition simply counts the number of tokens between two terms. The second definition is a logarithmic measure. The function returns the number of tokens from *a* to *b*; if *a* and *b* are adjacent, the count is 1; if *a* and *b* are separated by one token, the count is 2, and so on. A token can either be a character or a word; for the E-C, we used character-based tokenization, whereas for the E-J, we use word-based tokenization. By heuristics obtained from training results, we used the linear *Dist* measure for E-C and logarithmic *Dist* measure for E-J in the evaluation.

This algorithm is a simple statistical approach which requires no language-specific external tools beyond word segmentation and a named-entity tagger. It is not as sophisticated as other approaches which perform deep linguistic analysis, but one advantage is faster adaptation to multiple languages. In our experiments, this simple algorithm performs at the same level as a FST-based approach (Nyberg, et al. 2005).

3.5 Answer Generator

The task of the Answer Generator (AG) module is to produce a ranked list of answer candidates from the IX output. The AG is designed to normalize answer candidates by resolving representational differences (e.g. in how numbers, dates, etc. are expressed in text). This canonicalization makes it possible to combine answer candidates that differ only in surface form.

Even though the AG module plays an important role in JAVELIN, we did not use its full potential in our E-C and E-J systems, since we lacked some language-specific resources required for multilingual answer merging.

4 Evaluation and Effect of Translation Accuracy

To evaluate the effect of translation accuracy on the overall performance of the CLQA system, we conducted several experiments using different translation methods. Three different runs were carried out for both the E-C and E-J systems, using the same 200-question test set and the document corpora provided by the NTCIR CLQA task. The first run was a fully automatic run using the original translation module in the CLQA system; the result is exactly same as the one we submitted to NTCIR5 CLQA. For the second run, we manually translated the keywords that were selected by the Question Analyzer module. This translation was done by looking at only the selected keywords, but not the original question. For both E-C and E-J tasks, the NTCIR organizers provided the translations for the English questions, which we assume are the gold-standard translations. Taking advantage of this resource, in the third run we simply looked up the corresponding term for each English keyword from the gold-standard translation of the question. The results for these runs are shown in Table 7 and 8 below.

	Translation Accuracy	Top1	Top1+U
Run 1	69.3%	15 (7.5%)	23 (11.5%)
Run 2	85.5%	16 (8.0%)	31 (15.5%)
Run 3	100%	18 (9.0%)	38 (19.0%)

Table 7. Effect of Translation (E-C)

	Translation Accuracy	Top1	Top1+U
Run 1	54.2%	20 (10.0%)	25 (12.5%)
Run 2	81.2%	19 (9.5%)	30 (15.0%)
Run 3	100%	18 (9.0%)	31 (15.5%)

Table 8. Effect of Translation (E-J)

We found that in the NTCIR task, the supported/correct document set was not complete. Some answers judged as unsupported were indeed well supported, but the supporting document did not appear in NTCIR's correct document set. Therefore, we think the Top1+U column is more informative for this evaluation. From Table 7 and 8, it is obvious that the overall performance increases as translation accuracy increases. From Run1 to Run2, we eliminated all the overt translation errors produced by the system, and also corrected word-sense errors. Then from Run2 to Run3, we made different lexical choices among the seemingly all correct translations of a word. This type of inappropriateness cannot be classified as an error, but it makes a difference in QA systems, especially at the document retrieval stage. For example, the phrase "Kyoto Protocol" can have two valid translations: *京都協議* or *京都議定書*. Both translations would be understandable to a human, but the second translation will appear much more frequently than the first one in the document set. This type of lexical choice is hard to make, because we would need either subtle domain-specific knowledge, or knowledge about the target corpus; neither is easily obtainable.

Comparing Run 1 and 3 in Table 8, we see that improving keyword translation had less overall impact on the E-J system. Information extraction (including named entity identification) did not perform as well in E-J. We also compared the translation effect on cross-lingual document retrieval (Figure 3). As we can see, Run 3 retrieved supporting documents more frequently in rank 1 than in Run 1 or 2. From these preliminary investigations, it would seem that information extraction and/or answer generation must be improved for English-Japanese CLQA.

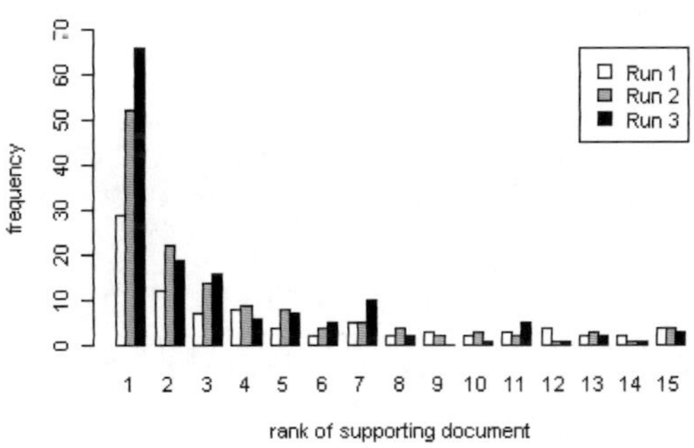

Figure3: Comparison of three runs: Cross-lingual document retrieval performance in E-J

5 Translation Issues

In this section, we discuss language specific keyword translation issues for Chinese and Japanese CLQA.

5.1 Chinese

One prominent problem in Chinese keyword translation is word sense disambiguation. In question answering systems, the translation results are used directly in information retrieval, which exhibits a high dependency on the lexical form of a word but not so much on the meaning. In other words, having a different lexical form from the corresponding term in corpora is the same as having a wrong translation. For example, to translate the word "bury" into Chinese, our system gives a translation of *埋*, which means "bury" as the action of digging a hole, hiding some items in the hole and then covering it with earth. But the desired translation, as it appears in the document is *葬*, which means "bury" too, but specifically for burial in funerals.

Even more challenging are regional language differences. In our system, for example, the corpora are newswire articles written in Traditional Chinese from Taiwan, and if we use an MT system that produces translations in Simplified Chinese followed by conversion to Traditional Chinese, we may run into problems. The MT system generates Simplified Chinese translations first, which may suggest that the translation resources it uses were written in Simplified Chinese and originate from mainland China. In mainland China and in Taiwan, people commonly use different words for describing the same thing, especially for proper nouns like foreign names. Table 9 lists some examples. Therefore if the MT system generates its output using text from mainland China, it may produce a different word than the one used in Taiwan, which may not appear in the corpora. This could lead to failure in document retrieval.

English	Mainland China	Taiwan
Band	樂隊	樂團
Computer Game	電腦遊戲	電玩
World Guinness Record	吉尼斯世界紀錄	金氏世界紀錄
The Catcher in the Rye	稻田裏的守望者	麥田捕手
Nelson	奈爾森	納爾遜
Salinger	塞林格	沙林傑
Creutzfeldt Jakob Disease	人類狂牛症	賈庫氏症
Luc Besson	呂克 貝松	盧貝松
Pavarotti	帕瓦洛蒂	帕華洛帝

Table 9. Different Translation in Chinese

5.2 Japanese

Representational Gaps: One of the advantages of using structured queries and automatic query formulation in the RS is that the system is able to handle slight representational gaps between a translated query and corresponding target words in the corpus.

For example, *Werner Spies* appears as *ヴェルナー・シュピース* in our Japanese preprocessed corpus and therefore *ヴェルナー シュピース*, which is missing a dot between last and first name, is a wrong translation if our retrieval module only allows exact match. Lemur supports an *Ordered Distance Operator* where the terms within a *#ODN* operator must be found within *N* words of each other in the text in order to contribute to the document's belief value. This enables us to bridge the representational gaps; such as when *#OD1(ヴェルナー シュピース)* does not match any words in the corpus, *#OD2(ヴェルナー シュピース)* is formulated in the next step in order to capture *ヴェルナー・シュピース*.

Transliteration in WBMT: After detecting Japanese nouns written in romaji (e.g. *Funabashi*), we transliterated them into hiragana for a better result in WBMT. This is because we are assuming higher positive co-occurrence between kana and kanji (i.e. *ふなばし* and *船橋*) than between romaji and kanji (i.e. *funabashi* and *船橋*). When there are multiple transliteration candidates, we iterate through each candidate.

Document Retrieval in Kana: Suppose we are going to transliterate *Yusuke*. This romaji can be mapped to kana characters with relatively less ambiguity (i.e. ゆすけ, ゆうすけ), when compared to their subsequent transliteration to kanji (i.e. *雄介*, *祐介*, *佑介*, *勇介*, *雄輔* etc.). Therefore, indexing kana readings in the corpus and querying in kana is sometimes a useful technique for CLQA, given the difficulty in converting romaji to kana and romaji to kanji.

To implement this approach, the Japanese corpus was first preprocessed by annotating named entities and by chunking morphemes. Then, we annotated a kana reading for each named entity. At query time, if there is no translation found from other resources, the TM transliterates romaji to kana as a back-off strategy.

6 Conclusion

We described how we extended an existing monolingual (English) system for CLQA (English to Chinese and English to Japanese), including a translation disambiguation technique which uses a noisy channel model with probability estimations using web as corpora. We discussed the influence of translation accuracy on CLQA by presenting experimental results and analysis. We concluded by introducing some language-specific issues for keyword translation from English to Chinese and Japanese which we hope to address in ongoing research.

Acknowledgements

This work is supported by the Advanced Research and Development Activity (ARDA)'s Advanced Question Answering for Intelligent (AQUAINT) Program.

References

Brown, P., J. Cocke, S.D. Pietra, V.D. Pietra, F. Jelinek., J. Lafferty, R. Mercer, and P. Roossin. 1990. A Statistical Approach to Machine Translation. *Computational Linguistics*, 16(2):38—45.

Isozaki, H., K. Sudoh and H. Tsukada. 2005. NTT's Japanese-English Cross-Language Question Answering System. In *Proceedings of the NTCIR Workshop 5 Meeting,* pages 186-193.

Korhonen, A. and E. Briscoe. 2004. Extended Lexical-Semantic Classification of English Verbs. *Proceedings of the HLT/NAACL '04 Workshop on Computational Lexical Semantics*, pages 38-45.

Kwok, K., P. Deng, N. Dinstl and S. Choi. 2005. NTCIR-5 English-Chinese Cross Language Question-Answering Experiments using PIRCS. In *Proceedings of the NTCIR Workshop 5 Meeting.*

Li, Hang, Yunbo Cao, and Cong Li. 2003. Using Bilingual Web Data To Mine and Rank Translations, *IEEE Intelligent Systems 18(4)*, pages 54-59.

Mori, T. and M. Kawagishi. 2005. A Method of Cross Language Question-Answering Based on Machine Translation and Transliteration. In *Proceedings of the NTCIR Workshop 5 Meeting.*

Nagata, N., T. Saito, and K. Suzuki. 2001. Using the Web as a Bilingual Dictionary, In *Proceedings of ACL 2001 Workshop Data-Driven Methods in Machine Translation,* pages 95-102

Nyberg, E., R. Frederking, T. Mitamura, J. M. Bilotti, K. Hannan, L. Hiyakumoto, J. Ko, F. Lin, L. Lita, V. Pedro, A. Schlaikjer. 2005. JAVELIN I and II in TREC2005. *In Proceedings of TREC 2005.*

Ogilvie, P. and J. Callan. 2001. Experiments Using the Lemur Toolkit. In *Proceedings of the 2001 Text REtrieval Conference (TREC 2001)*, pages 103-108.

Turney, P.D. 2001, Mining the Web for synonyms: PMI-IR versus LSA on TOEFL, *Proceedings of the Twelfth European Conference on Machine Learning*, pages 491-502.

BRUJA: Question Classification for Spanish. Using Machine Translation and an English Classifier.

Miguel Á. García Cumbreras
SINAI Group
Computer Sciences
University of Jaén. Spain
magc@ujaen.es

L. Alfonso Ureña López
SINAI Group
Computer Sciences
University of Jaén. Spain
laurena@ujaen.es

Fernando Martínez Santiago
SINAI Group
Computer Sciences
University of Jaén .Spain
dofer@ujaen.es

Abstract

Question Classification is an important task in Question Answering Systems. This paper presents a Spanish Question Classifier based on machine learning, automatic online translators and different language features. Our system works with English collections and bilingual questions (English/Spanish). We have tested two Spanish-English online translators to identify the lost of precision. We have made experiments using lexical, syntactic and semantic features to test which ones made a better performance. The obtained results show that our system makes good classifications, over a 80% in terms of accuracy using the original English questions and over a 65% using Spanish questions and machine translation systems. Our conclusion about the features is that a lexical, syntactic and semantic features combination obtains the best result.

1 Introduction

A Question Answering (QA) system seeks and shows the user an accurate and concise answer, given a free-form question, and using a large text data collection.

The use of Cross Language Information Retrieval Systems (CLIR) is growing, and also the application of these ones into other general systems, such as Question Answering or Question Classification.

A CLIR system is an Information Retrieval System that works with collections in several languages, and extract relevant documents or passages (Grefenstette, 1998).

We have proposed a Multilingual Question Answering System (BRUJA - in Spanish "Busqueda de Respuestas University of Jaen") that works with collections in several languages. Since there are several languages, tasks such as obtaining relevant documents and extracting the answer could be accomplished in two ways: using NPL tools and resources for each language or for a pivot language only (English) and translating to the pivot language the rest of the relevant information when it is required. Because of the translation step, the second approach is less accurate but more practical since we need only NPL resources for English. The central question is the noise, because of the translation process, is too high in order to use this approach in spite of their practical advantages.

The first step of this system is a Question Classifier (QC). Given a query, a question classification module obtains the class of such question. This information is useful for the extraction of the answer. For example, given the query "Where is Madrid?, the QA system expects a location entity as answer type. The proposed QA module works with questions in several languages, translates them into English using different online translators, and obtains the type of questions and some features, such as the focus, the keywords or the context. In this work we aim to find out whether a multilingual QC module is possible by using translation tools and English as pivot language or not.

2 Question Classification

Question Classification is the task that, given a question, classifies it in one of *k* semantic classes.

Some QC systems are based on regular expressions and manual grammatical rules (Van Durme et al., 2003).

Recent works in QC have studied different machine learning methods. (Zhang and Lee, 2003) propose a QC system that uses Support Vector Machine (SVM) as the best machine learning algorithm. They compare the obtained results with other algorithms, such as Nearest Neighbors, Naive Bayes, Decision Tree or Sparse Network of Winnows (SNoW).

(Li and Roth, 2002) propose a system based on SNoW. They used five main classes and fifty fined classes. Other systems have used SVM and modified kernels.

QC systems have some restrictions (Hacioglu and Ward, 2003), such as:

- Traditional question classification uses a set of rules, for instance "questions that start with *Who* ask about a person". These are manual rules that have to be revised to improve the results.
- These rules are very weak, because when new questions arise, the system has to be updated to classify them.

Most of the QC systems use English as the main language, and some of the best and standard resources are developed for English.

It would be possible to build a question classifier for every language based on machine learning, using a good training corpus for each language, but is something expensive to produce. For this reason we have used Machine Translation Systems.

Machine Translation (MT) systems are very appreciated in CLIR (McNamee et al., 2000). Last years these systems have improved the results, but there are not translators for each language pair and the quality of the result depends on this pair.

The reason of using MT and not a Spanish classifier is simple: we have developed a multilingual QA system that works in this moment with three languages: English, Spanish and French. Because it is too complex for us to work with resources into these three languages and also to manage the information into three languages, our kernel system works into English, and we use MT to translate information when it is necessary.

We have developed a QC system that covers three tasks:

- It uses machine learning algorithms. We have tested methods based on Support Vector Machine, for instance SVMLight or LibSVM, and TiMBL. TiMBL [1] is a program that implements several Memory-Based Learning techniques. It stores a representation of the training set explicitly in memory, and classifies new cases by extrapolation from the most similar stored cases.
- To classify Spanish questions we have checked two online machine translators. Our proposal is to study how the translation can affect in the final results, compared to the original English results.
- Finally, we would obtain different results applying different levels of features (lexical, syntactic and semantic). In the next section well explain them and in results chapter we will see these differences.

Our QC system has three independent modules, so it will be easy to replace each one with other to improve the final results. In Figure 1 we can see them.

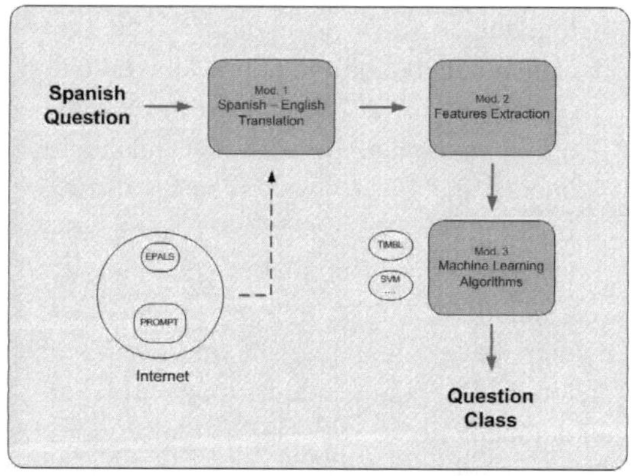

Figure 1: QC system Modules.

The first module translates the question into other languages, Spanish in this case. We have used two machine translation systema that work well for the language pair Spanish-English: Epals and Prompt. This module could work with other machine translation systems and other languages if there would be a good translator for the language pair used.

The second module extracts some relevant features (see next section) using the original or the translated English questions. Some of these features will be used by the machine learning module (lexical, syntactic and semantic features) and the

[1] ILK Research Group, Tilburg University and CNTS Research Group, University of Antwerp

others will be used later in the answers extraction phase. Take into account that the second module also extracts important features such as the context of the question, the focus or the keywords that we would use in next steps of the Question Answering system.

The final module applies the machine learning algorithm and returns the question category or class. In our first experiments we used Library for Support Vector Machines (LibSVM) and Bayesian Logistic Regression (BBR), but for this one we have used Tilburg Memory Based Learner (TiMBL).

TiMBL (Daelemans et al., 2004) implements several Memory-Based Learning techniques, classic k-NN classification kernel and several metrics. It implements Stanfill modified value difference metric (MVDM), Jeffrey Divergence and Class voting in the k-NN kernel according to the distance of the nearest neighbors. It makes classification using heuristic approximations, such as the IGTREE decision tree algorithm and the TRIBL and TRIBL2 hybrids. It also has optimizations for fast classification.

2.1 Features in Question Classification

We have analyzed each question in order to extract the following features:

- Lexical Features
  - The two first words of the question
  - All the words of the question in lowercase
  - The stemming words
  - Bigrams of the question
  - Each word with its position in the question
  - The interrogative pronoun of the question
  - The headwords of the nouns and verbs
- Syntactic Features
  - The interrogative pronoun and the Part of Speech (POS) of the rest of the words
  - The headword (a word to which an independent meaning can be assigned) of the first noun phrase
  - All POS
  - Chunks
  - The first verb chunk
  - The length of the question
- Semantic Features
  - The question focus (a noun phrase that is likely to be present in the answer)
  - POS with the named entities recognized
  - The type of the entity if the focus is one of them
  - Wordnet hypernyms for the nouns and Wordnet synonyms for the verbs

We have used some English resources such as the POS tagger TreeTagger (Schmid, 1994), Lingpipe [2] to make Named Entity Recognition, and the Porter stemmer (Porter, 1980). We have also used Wordnet to expand the queries.

3 Experiments and Results

3.1 Experimental Method

The experiments are made using some public datasets available by USC (Hovy et al., 1999), UIUC and TREC [3] as training and test collections.

These datasets have been labeled manually by UIUC group by means of the following general and detailed categories:

ABBR: abbreviation, expansion.

DESC: definition, description, manner, reason.

ENTY: animal, body, color, creation, currency, disease/medical, event, food, instrument, language, letter, other, plant, product, religion, sport, substance, symbol, technique, term, vehicle, word.

HUM: description, group, individual, title.

LOC: city, country, mountain, other, state.

NUM: code, count, date, distance, money, order, other, percent, period, speed, temperature, size, weight.

For instance the question "*What does NATO mean?*" is an ABBR (abbreviation) category, "*What is a receptionist?*" is a DESC (definition) category or "*When did George Bush born?*" is a NUM (numeric) category.

The training data are a set of 5500 questions and the test data are a set of 500 questions. All questions were labelled for the 10th conference Cross-Language Evaluation Forum of Question Answering (CLEF-QA).

[2] LingPipe is a suite of Java tools designed to perform linguistic analysis on natural language data, available in http://www.alias-i.com/lingpipe

[3] http://trec.nist.gov

The same dataset has been used in other investigations, such as in (Li and Roth, 2002).

The distribution of these 5500 training questions, with respect to its interrogative pronoun or the initial word is showed in Table 1.

Likewise, the distribution of categories of these 5500 training questions is showed in Table 2.

Table 1: Training questions distribution according with its interrogative pronoun

Type	Number
What	3242
Who	577
How	764
Where	273
When	131
Which	105
Why	103
Name	91
In	67
Define	4
Whom	4
Others	91

Table 2: Training questions distribution according with its general category.

Category	Number
ABBR	86
DESC	1162
ENTY	1251
HUM	1223
LOC	835
NUM	896

The distribution of the 500 test questions, with respect to its interrogative pronoun or the initial word, is showed in Table 3, and the distribution of categories of these 500 test questions is showed in Table 4.

Table 3: Test questions distribution according with its interrogative pronoun.

Type	Number
What	343
Who	47
How	35
Where	26
When	26
Which	6
Why	4
Name	2
In	5
Others	6

In our experiments we try to identify the general category. Our proposal is to try a detailed classification later.

Table 4: Test questions distribution according with its general category.

Category	Number
ABBR	9
DESC	138
ENTY	94
HUM	65
LOC	81
NUM	113

We have used the Accuracy as a general measure and the Precision of each category as a detailed measure.

$$Accuracy = \frac{\sharp of correct predictions}{\sharp of predictions} \quad (1)$$

$$precision(\mathbf{c}) = \frac{\sharp of correct predictions of the category c}{\sharp of predictions of the category c} \quad (2)$$

Other measure used is the F-score, defined as the harmonic mean of precision and recall (Van Rijsbergen, 1979). It is a commonly used metric to summarize precision and recall in one measure.

$$F - score = \frac{2 * precision * recall}{precision + recall} \quad (3)$$

3.2 Results

We have made some experiments changing the machine translation systems:

- 5500 training questions and 500 test questions, all into English. This is the basic case.
- 5500 training questions into English and 500 test questions translated from Spanish using the MT Epals.
- 5500 training questions into English and 500 test questions translated from Spanish using the MT Prompt.

The MT resources are available in the following URLs:

- *Epals*

  http://www.epals.com
- *Prompt*

  http://translation2.paralink.com

According to the lexical, syntactic and semantic features we have made seven features sets. Our proposal here is to check which ones increase the final results. These features sets are the following:

1. Lexical Features: interrogative pronoun *(lex1)*

2. Lexical and Syntactic Features: Two first words of the question + All the words of the question in lowercase + Stemming words + Headwords *(lexsyn2)*

3. Lexical and Syntactic Features: previous four + Each word with its position in the question + interrogative pronoun + The first verb chunk *(lexsyn3)*

4. Semantic Features: The question focus + POS with the named entities recognized + The type of the entity if the focus is one of them *(sem4)*

5. Syntactic Features: The interrogative pronoun and the Part of Speech (POS) of the rest of the words + All POS + Chunks + The length of the question *(sin5)*

6. All Lexical + all Syntactic + all Semantic *(lexsemsin6)*

7. Lexical Features: Two first words of the question + interrogative pronoun ; Syntactic Features: + The headwords of the nouns and verbs + The first verb chunk + the interrogative pronoun + the Part of Speech (POS) of the rest of the words + The length of the question; Semantic Features: POS with the named entities recognized *(lexsemsin7)*

We can see in the Table 5 the obtained results in terms of global accuracy.

Table 5: Results in terms of Accuracy.

Features	English original	Epals	Prompt
lex1	0,458	0,334	0,414
lexsyn2	0,706	0,656	0,632
lexsyn3	0,718	0,638	0,612
sem4	0,675456	0,59798	0,629555
sin5	0,608	0,438	0,518
lexsemsin6	0,839757	0,662626	0,722672
lexsemsin7	0,8	0,678	0,674

Note that the average loss of precision is around 17% if we use Epals, and around 12% if we use Prompt.

(Li and Roth, 2002) obtain a better performance for English, around a 92.5% in terms of accuracy.

The best results are obtained when we use a combination of all lexical, syntactic and semantic features. The main reason is that the classifier works better when the number of features, which can be different to each category, is increased.

For future work, it will be also necessary to study the time consumption for each features set, to decide which ones can be used.

Table 6 shows the results in terms of F-score.

Table 6: Results in terms of F-score.

Features	English original	Epals	Prompt
lex1	0,476077	0,319793	0,441075
lexsyn2	0,708444	0,669692	0,6455
lexsyn3	0,721258	0,644813	0,614353
sem4	0,649405	0,593019	0,620068
sin5	0,576356	0,404038	0,48739
lexsemsin6	0,827789	0,664122	0,726667
lexsemsin7	0,795897	0,680039	0,68014

As an example in Table 7 we show detailed results for the best case, where the result for each general category is showed.

Table 7: Detailed results for each category, using the combination *lexsemsin6* and the original English questions and the translated questions by using Prompt

Class	English original		Prompt	
	Precision	*F-score*	*Precision*	*F-score*
ABBR	0.857	0.750	1	0.611
DESC	0.8442	0.906	0.695	0.806
ENTY	0.731	0.727	0.595	0.737
HUM	0.839	0.825	0.898	0.914
LOC	0.847	0.867	0.680	0.859
NUM	0.935	0.843	0.798	0.856

As we have seen there are no important differences between categories. In addition, this table shows that the translation results are reliable since for every category the lost of precision is similar (about 15%).

There are some reasons for the lost of precision. Some of them are the following:

1. Bad translation of synonym words. For instance we can compare an English original sentence: "What are the animals that don't have backbones called?", and its Prompt translation: "How are they called the animals that have no spines?". The word *backbone* has been replaced with *spine*, so the IR system cannot find the same lists of relevant documents.

2. Translation of Named Entities. For instance we can compare an English original sentence: "Who was Galileo?", and its Prompt translation: "Who was Galilean?".

3. General bad translations. For instance we can compare an English original sentence: "Who discovered x-rays?", and its Prompt translation: "Who discovered the beams the Xth?".

4 Conclusions

Multilingual Question Answering systems have opened a new investigation task, where the question classification is an important first phase to know the type of answer and some relevant information about this question.

Our option is to use some standards resources for English and translate Spanish questions.

Of course we could develop a multilingual QC system using good training corpus for every language, but it is expensive to produce.

The use of machine translation systems is, then, very important, so the study of different online translators is a main task. In our case we have applied them to translate questions from Spanish into English.

We have made a complete investigation using the two datasets of training and test questions that have been used by other groups, all labelled manually. Different parameters have been the test file used (originally in English or translated from Spanish with the MT Epals or Prompt), the machine learning algorithm, some TiMBL parameters and the lexical, syntactic or semantic features.

The best results have been obtained using the original English questions and a combination of lexical, syntactic and semantic features. The best MT has been Prompt.

We have some conclusions:

- Applying machine learning with a complete set of training questions we obtain good results, over 0,8 in terms of accuracy.
- The use of machine translation systems decreases the results around 15%, but it will be possible to increase the performance using other models based on machine learning or a voting system for instance.
- A combination of all lexical, syntactic and semantic features obtains the best results.

As future work we want to check the system with other training and test datasets. We also want to design a voting system using different QC models; models based on patterns (to detect the class for some types of questions); models based on rules (filtering non-redundancy types of questions. For instance all questions with "who" are related to a person).

It could be also interested to test the combination between a better QC system, the current one by Li and Roths for instance (Li and Roth, 2002), and our machine translation method.

Finally, we want to study types of questions with poor results in order to improve them applying other techniques, such as question expansion.

Acknowledgement This work has been supported by Spanish Government (MCYT) with grant TIC2003-07158-C04-04.

References

W. Daelemans, J. Zavrel, K. van der Sloot, and A. van den Bosch. 2004. Timbl: Tilburgmemory based learner, version 5.1, reference guide. ilk technical report 04-02.

G. Grefenstette, editor. 1998. *Cross-Language Information Retrieval*, volume 1. Kluwer academic publishers, Boston, USA.

K. Hacioglu and W. Ward. 2003. Question classification with support vector machines and error correcting codes. In *Proceedings of Human Language Technology conference (HLT-NAACL)*.

E. Hovy, L. Gerber, U. Hermjakob, C. Lin, and D. Ravichandran. 1999. Towards sematics-based answer pinpointing. In *Proceedings of the DARPA Human Language Technology conference (HLT)*.

X. Li and D. Roth. 2002. Learning question classifiers. In *In COLING'02*.

P. McNamee, J. Mayfield, and C. Piatko. 2000. The jhu/apl haircut system at trec- 8. In *Proceedings of the Eighth Text Retrieval Conference (TREC8)*.

M. F. Porter. 1980. An algorithm for suffix stripping. In *Program 14*.

H. Schmid. 1994. Probabilistic part-of-speech tagging using decision trees. In *Proceedings of International Conference on New Methods in Language Processing*.

B. Van Durme, Y. Huang, A. Kupsc, and E. Nyberg. 2003. Towards light semantic processing for question answering. In *Proceedings of Human Language Technology conference (HLT-NAACL)*.

C.J. Van Rijsbergen. 1979. Information retrieval.

D. Zhang and W. Sun Lee. 2003. Question classification using support vector machines. In *Proceedings of the 26th Annual International ACM SIGIR Conference on Research and Development in Information Retrieval*.

Monolingual Web-based Factoid Question Answering in Chinese, Swedish, English and Japanese

E.W.D. Whittaker **J. Hamonic** **D. Yang** **T. Klingberg** **S. Furui**
Dept. of Computer Science
Tokyo Institute of Technology
2-12-1, Ookayama, Meguro-ku
Tokyo 152-8552 Japan
{edw,yuuki,raymond,tor,furui}@furui.cs.titech.ac.jp

Abstract

In this paper we extend the application of our statistical pattern classification approach to question answering (QA) which has previously been applied successfully to English and Japanese to develop two prototype QA systems in Chinese and Swedish. We show what data is necessary to achieve this and also evaluate the performance of the two new systems using a translation of the TREC 2003 factoid QA task. While performance for Chinese and Swedish is found to be lower than that for the more developed English and Japanese systems we explain why this is the case and offer solutions for their improvement. All systems form the basis of our publicly accessible web-based multilingual QA system at `http://asked.jp`.

1 Introduction

Much of the research into automatic question answering (QA) has understandably concentrated on the English language with little regard to portability or efficacy in other languages. It is only relatively recently, with the introduction of the CLEF and NTCIR QA evaluations, that researchers have started to look at porting and evaluating the techniques that have been shown to work well for English to other languages.

One of the major drawbacks of porting an English language QA system or approach to other languages is often the lack of the corresponding NLP tools in the target language. For instance, parsers and named-entity (NE)-taggers, which are typical components in many QA systems, are certainly not available for all the world's languages. Trainable parsers and NE-taggers similarly require appropriate training data which, if not available, is costly and requires specialized knowledge to produce. Language-specific databases are also a common feature of many systems, some of which have taken many man-years to construct and verify. Such a component in many English-language systems, for example, is WordNet. While porting WordNet to other languages has been started in the Euro and Global WordNet projects they still only cover a relatively small number of languages.

In this paper we describe the application of our data-driven approach to QA which was developed right from the outset with the aim of portability and robustness in mind. This statistical pattern classification approach to QA is essentially language independent and trainable given appropriate language-specific training data. No assumptions about the language are made by the model except that some notion of words or space-separated tokens must exist or be introduced where it is absent. Our only other requirements to build a QA system in a new target language are: a large collection of text data in the target language that can be searched for answers (e.g. the web), and a list of example questions-and-answers (q-and-a) in the target language. Given these data sources the remaining components can be obtained automatically for each language.

So, in contrast to other contemporary approaches to QA our English language system does not use WordNet as in (Hovy et al., 2001; Moldovan et al., 2002), NE extraction, or any other linguistic information e.g. from semantic analysis (Hovy et al., 2001) or from question parsing (Hovy et al., 2001; Moldovan et al., 2002) and uses capitalised (where appropriate for the language) word tokens as the only features for modelling. For our Japanese system, although we currently use Chasen to segment Japanese character sequences into units that resemble words, we make no use of any morphological information as used for example in (Fuchigami et al., 2004). Moreover, it should be noted that our approach is at the same time very different to other purely web-based approaches such as askMSR (Brill et al., 2002) and Aranea (Lin et al., 2002). For example, we use entire documents rather than the snippets of text returned by web search engines; we do not use structured document sources or databases and we do not transform the query in any way either by term re-ordering or by modifying the tense of verbs. These basic principles apply to each of our language-specific QA systems thus simplifying and accelerating development.

The approach to QA that we adopt has previously been described in (Whittaker et al., 2005a; Whittaker et al., 2005b; Whittaker et al., 2005c) where the details of the mathematical model and how it was trained for English and Japanese were given. Our approach has also been successfully evaluated in the text retrieval conference (TREC) 2005 QA track evaluation (Voorhees, 2003) where our group placed eleventh out of thirty participants (Whittaker et al., 2005a). Although the TREC QA task is substantially different to web-based QA the TREC evaluation confirmed that our approach works and also provides an objective assessment of its quality. Similarly, for our Japanese language system we have previously evaluated the performance of our approach on the NTCIR-3 QAC-1 task (Whittaker et al., 2005c). Although our Japanese experiments were applied retrospectively, the results would have placed us in the mid-range of participating systems in that year's evaluation. In this paper we present additional experiments on Chinese and Swedish and explain how our statistical pattern classification approach to QA was successfully applied to these two new languages. Using our approach and given appropriate training data it is found that a reasonably proficient developer can build a QA system in a new language in around 10 hours. Evaluation of the Chinese and Swedish systems is performed using a translation of the first 200 factoid questions from the TREC 2003 evaluation which we have also made available online. We compare these results both qualitatively and quantitatively against results obtained previously for English and Japanese. The systems, built using this method, form the basis of our multi-language web demo which is publicly available at `http://asked.jp`.

An outline of the remainder of this paper is as follows: we briefly describe our statistical pattern classification approach to QA in Section 2 repeating the important elements of our approach as necessary to understand the remainder of the paper. In Section 3 we describe the basic building blocks of our QA system and how they can typically be trained. We also give a breakdown of the data used to train each language specific QA system. In Section 4 we present the results of experiments on Chinese, Swedish, English and Japanese and in Section 5 we compare and analyse these results. We wrap up with a conclusion and further work in Sections 6 and 7.

2 Statistical pattern classification approach to QA

The answer to a question depends primarily on the question itself but also on many other factors such as the person asking the question, the location of the person, what questions the person has asked before, and so on. Although such factors are clearly relevant in a real-world scenario they are difficult to model and also to test in an off-line mode, for example, in the context of the NTCIR and TREC evaluations. We therefore choose to consider only the dependence of an answer A on the question Q, where each is considered to be a string of l_A words $A = a_1, \ldots, a_{l_A}$ and l_Q words $Q = q_1, \ldots, q_{l_Q}$, respectively. In particular, we hypothesize that the answer A depends on two sets of features $W = \mathcal{W}(Q)$ and $X = \mathcal{X}(Q)$ as follows:

$$P(A \mid Q) = P(A \mid W, X), \qquad (1)$$

where $W = w_1, \ldots, w_{l_W}$ can be thought of as a set of l_W features describing the "question-type" part of Q such as *who, when, where, which,* etc. and $X = x_1, \ldots, x_{l_X}$ is a set of l_X features comprising the "information-bearing" part of Q i.e. what the question is actually about and what it refers to. For example, in the questions, *"Where was Tom Cruise married?"* and *"When was Tom Cruise married?"* the information-bearing component is identical in both cases whereas the question-type component is different.

Finding the best answer $\hat{A}$ involves a search over all A for the one which maximizes the probability of the above model:

$$\hat{A} = \arg\max_{A} P(A \mid W, X). \qquad (2)$$

Using Bayes rule, making further conditional independence assumptions and assuming uniform prior probabilities, which therefore do not affect the optimisation criterion, we obtain the final optimisation criterion (see (Whittaker et al., 2005a) for more details):

$$\arg\max_{A} \underbrace{P(A \mid X)}_{\substack{retrieval\\ model}} \cdot \underbrace{P(W \mid A)}_{\substack{filter\\ model}}. \qquad (3)$$

The $P(A \mid X)$ model is essentially a language model which models the probability of an answer sequence A given a set of information-bearing features X. It models the proximity of A to features in X. We call this model the *retrieval model* and examine it further in Section 2.1.

The $P(W \mid A)$ model matches an answer A with features in the question-type set W. Roughly speaking this model relates ways of asking a question with classes of valid answers. For example, it associates dates, or days of the week with *when*-type questions. In general, there are many valid and equiprobable A for a given W so this component can only re-rank candidate answers retrieved by the retrieval model. Consequently, we call it the *filter model* and examine it further in Section 2.2.

2.1 Retrieval model

The retrieval model essentially models the proximity of A to features in X. Since $A = a_1, \ldots, a_{l_A}$ we are actually modelling the distribution of multi-word sequences. This should be borne in mind in the following discussion whenever A is used. As mentioned above, we currently use a deterministic information-feature mapping function $X = \mathcal{X}(Q)$. This mapping only generates word m-tuples ($m = 1, 2, \ldots$) from single words in Q that are not present in a *stoplist* of 50-100 high-frequency words. For more details on the exact form of the retrieval model please refer to (Whittaker et al., 2005a).

2.2 Filter model

A set of $|V_{\mathcal{W}}|$ single-word features is extracted based on frequency of occurrence in question data. Some examples include: *HOW*, *MANY*, *WHEN*, *WHO*, *UNTIL* etc. The question-type mapping function $\mathcal{W}(Q)$ extracts n-tuples ($n = 1, 2, \ldots$) of question-type features from the question Q, such as *HOW MANY* and *UNTIL WHEN*.

Modelling the complex relationship between W and A directly is non-trivial. We therefore introduce an intermediate variable representing classes of example questions-and-answers (q-and-a) c_e for $e = 1 \ldots |C_E|$ drawn from the set C_E, and to facilitate modelling we say that W is conditionally independent of A given c_e as follows:

$$P(W \mid A) = \sum_{e=1}^{|C_E|} P(W \mid c_e) \cdot P(c_e \mid A). \qquad (4)$$

Given a set E of example q-and-a t_j for $j = 1 \ldots |E|$ where $t_j = (q^j, a^j) = (q_1^j, \ldots, q_{l_{Qj}}^j, a_1^j, \ldots, a_{l_{Aj}}^j)$ we define a mapping function $f : E \rightarrow C_E$ by $f(t_j) = e$. Each class $c_e = (w_1^e, \ldots, w_{l_{We}}^e, a_1^e, \ldots, a_{l_{Ae}}^e)$ is then obtained by $c_e = \bigcup_{j:f(t_j)=e} \mathcal{W}(q^j) \bigcup_{i=1}^{l_{Aj}} a_i^j$. In all the experiments in this paper no clustering of the q-and-a is actually performed so each q-and-a example forms its own unique class i.e. each c_e corresponds to a single t_j and vice-versa.

Assuming conditional independence of the answer words in class c_e given A and making the modelling assumption that the jth answer word a_j^e in the example class c_e is dependent only on the jth answer word in A we obtain:

$$P(W \mid A) = \sum_{e=1}^{|C_E|} P(W \mid c_e) \cdot \prod_{j=1}^{l_{Ae}} P(a_j^e \mid a_j)$$
$$= \sum_{e=1}^{|C_E|} P(W \mid c_e) \prod_{j=1}^{l_{Ae}} \sum_{a=1}^{|C_A|} P(a_j^e \mid c_a) P(c_a \mid a_j), \qquad (5)$$

where c_a is a concrete class in the set of $|C_A|$ answer classes C_A, and assuming a_j^e is conditionally independent of c_a given a_j. The system using the formulation of filter model given by Equation (5) is referred to as model ONE. The model given by Equation (4) is referred to as model TWO, however, we are only concerned with model ONE in this paper.

Answer typing, such as it exists in our model ONE system, is performed by the filter model and is effected by matching the input query against our set of example questions C_E. Each one of these example questions c_e has an answer associated with it which in turn is expanded via the C_A classes into a set of possible answers for each question. At each step this matching process is entirely probabilistic as given by Equation (5). To take a simple example, if we are presented with the input query *"Who was the U.S. President who first used Camp David?"* the first step effectively matches the words (and bigrams, trigrams) in that query against the words (and bigrams, trigrams) in our example questions with a probability of its match assigned to all example questions. Suppose, for example, that the top-scoring example question in our set is *"Who was the U.S. President who resigned as a result of the Watergate affair?"* since the first six words in each question match each other and will likely result in a high probability being assigned. The corresponding answer to this example question is *"Richard Nixon"*. So the next step expands *"Richard"* using C_A and results in a high score being assigned to a class of words which tend to share the feature of being male first names, one of which is *"Franklin"*. Expanding the second word in the answer *"Nixon"* using C_A will possibly result in a high score being assigned to a class of words that share the feature of being the surnames of U.S. presidents, one of which is *"Roosevelt"*. In this way, we end up with a high score assigned by the filter model to *"Franklin Roosevelt"* but also to *"Abraham Lincoln"*, *"Bill Clinton"*, etc. In combination with the retrieval model, we hope that the documents obtained for this query assign a higher retrieval model score to *"Franklin Roosevelt"* over the names of other U.S. presidents and thus output it in first place with the highest overall probability. While this approach works well for names, dates and short place names it does fall down, for example, on names of books, plays and films where there is typically less of a clear correspondence between the words in any given position of two answers. This situation could be avoided by using multi-word answer strings and not making the position-dependence modelling assumption that was made to arrive at Equation (5) but this has its own drawbacks.

The above description of the operation of the filter model highlights the need for homogeneous classes of C_A of sufficiently wide coverage. In the next section we describe a way in which this can be achieved in an efficient, data-driven manner for essentially any language.

2.3 Obtaining C_A

As we saw in the previous section the C_A are the closest thing we have to named entities since they define classes of words that share some similarity with each other. However, in some sense they are more flexible than named entities since any word can actually belong to any class but with a certain probability. In this way we don't rule out with a zero probability the possibility of a word belonging to some class, just that a word is more likely to belong to some classes than others. In addition, the entities are not actually named i.e. we do not impose our own label on the classes so we do not explicitly have a class of first names, or a class of days of the week. Although we hope that we will end up with classes containing such similar words we do not make it explicit and we do not label what each class of words is supposed to represent.

In keeping with our data-driven philosophy and related objective to make our approach as language-independent as possible we use an agglomerative clustering algorithm to derive classes automatically from data. The set of potential answer words V_{C_A} that are clustered, should ideally cover all possible words that might ever be answers to questions. We therefore take the most frequent $|V_{C_A}|$ words from a language-specific corpus T comprising $|T|$ word tokens as our set of potential answers. The "seeds" for the clusters are chosen to be the most frequent $|C_A|$ words in T. The algorithm then uses the co-occurrence probabilities of words in T to group together words with similar co-occurrence statistics. For each word a in V_{C_A} the co-occurrence probability $P(a_i \mid a, d)$ is the probability of a_i given a occurring d words away. If d is positive, a_i occurs after a, and if negative, before a. We then construct a vector of co-occurrences with maximum separation between words D, as follows:

$$\vec{a} = [P(a_1 \mid a, 1), \ldots, P(a_R \mid a, 1), P(a_1 \mid a, -1), \ldots, P(a_R \mid a, -1), \ldots\ldots, P(a_1 \mid a, D), \ldots, P(a_R \mid a, D), P(a_1 \mid a, -D), \ldots, P(a_R \mid a, -D)]. \quad (6)$$

Rather than storing $2DV_{C_A}^2$ elements we can compute most terms efficiently and on-the-fly using

Language	T	$\|T\|$	$\|V_{C_A}\|$	$\|C_E\|$	$\|C_A\|$
Chinese	TREC Mandarin (Rogers, 2000)	68M	33k	7k	1000
Swedish	PAROLE (University, 1997)	19M	367k	5k	1000
English	AQUAINT (Voorhees, 2002)	300M	215k	290k	500
Japanese	MAINICHI (Fukumoto et al., 2002)	150M	300k	270k	5000

Table 1: Description of each of the four monolingual QA systems.

the Katz back-off method (Katz, 1987) and absolute discounting for estimating the probabilities of unobserved events. To find the distance between two vectors, for efficiency, we use an L_1 distance metric: $\mathcal{D}(\vec{a_i}, \vec{a_j}) = |\vec{a_i} - \vec{a_j}|$. Merging two vectors then involves a straightforward update of the co-occurrence counts for a cluster and recomputing the affected conditional probabilities and back-off weights. The clustering algorithm is described below:

Algorithm 2.1 Cluster words to generate C_A

```
initialize most frequent words to |C_A|
   classes
for i:= 1 to |V_{C_A}|
   for j:= 1 to |C_A|
        compute D(a_i, c_j)
   move a_i to c_j^best
   update c_j^best
```

Although the algorithm is currently applied offline before system deployment it could also be easily adapted to handle multi-word sequences and could also be applied at run-time thus reducing the effects of out-of-vocabulary answers.

3 System components

There are four basic ingredients to building a QA system using our approach: (1) a collection of example q-and-a (C_E) pairs used for answer-typing (answers need not necessarily be correct but must be of the correct answer type); (2) a classification of words (or word-like units cf. Japanese/Chinese) into classes of similar words (C_A) e.g. a class of country names, of given names, of numbers etc.; (3) a list of question words (*qlist*) such as *"WHO"*, *"WHERE"*, *"WHEN"* etc.; and (4) a stop list of words that should be ignored by the retrieval model (*stoplist*) as described in Section 2.1.

The q-and-a (C_E) for different languages can often be found on the web or in commercial quiz software. To date, we have not examined how many or what distribution of types of example q-and-a are important for good performance. However, intuitively, one expects that the richer and more varied the questions the better the performance will be. For the time being we aim to include as many examples as possible and hope this covers the kinds of questions that are asked in reality (or at least in the evaluations). In principle, in a working system it should also be possible to feed a user's question together with the user's response back into the system to improve performance in an unsupervised manner, so that performance would gradually improve over time.

To obtain the classes of answers C_A for each language Algorithm 2.1 is applied. The qlist is generated by taking the most frequently occurring terms from the question portion of the example q-and-a. The stoplist is formed from the 50-100 most frequently occurring words in T.

Google is used to retrieve documents for all questions, except Japanese, where an index of the NTCIR 2001 web snapshot is used instead. The question is passed as-is to Google after the removal of stop words. The top U documents are downloaded in their entirety, HTML markup removed, the text cleaned and upper-cased (where appropriate). For consistency, all data in our system is encoded using UTF-8.

The data source and relevant system details for each language-specific QA system are given in Table 1. For the Japanese system Chasen[1] is used to segment character sequences into word-like units. For Chinese each sentence is mapped to a sequence of space-separated characters.

4 Experimental work

A substantial amount of time has gone into investigating combinations and ranges of parameters which gave good performance on English development questions. These same parameters were largely used as-is for the Japanese system with only minor optimisations performed on de-

[1]`http://chasen.naist.jp/hiki/ChaSen`

Top Answers	Chinese "TREC 2003"	Swedish "TREC 2003"	English		Japanese QAC-1
			TREC 2003	TREC 2005	
1	14 (7%)	23 (11.5%)	99 (24.0%)	64 (17.7%)	37 (18.5%)
5	24 (12.0%)	34 (17.0%)	175 (42.4%)	121 (33.4%)	61 (30.5%)
10	33 (16.5%)	46 (23.0%)	196 (47.5%)	151 (41.7%)	69 (34.5%)
20	39 (19.5%)	50 (25.0%)	216 (52.3%)	167 (46.1%)	81 (40.5%)
Total Questions	200	200	413	362	200

Table 2: Performance of each language-specific system in the top 1, 5, 10 and 20 answers output.

velopment questions disjoint from any evaluation set. For the two new QA systems in Chinese and Swedish we used exactly the same parameters that had been found to work well for the English system and performed no optimisation, mainly due to a lack of questions that we could hold-out for development. This is clearly sub-optimal but will be addressed in future work.

It has been found for English and Japanese that system performance consistently increases the more documents that are used to search for an answer. Experiments with English used $U = 500$ documents and for Japanese $U = 5000$ documents was used. Due to time constraints, however, for the Swedish experiments we used a maximum of $U = 100$ documents. For the Chinese experiments we were forced to use a maximum of only $U = 20$ documents. This was because the segmentation of Chinese text into individual characters resulted in a huge number of character combinations being generated in the retrieval model and due to memory limitations the only way round this problem was to limit the number of documents used. In addition, for an answer to be output the number of times it had to occur in the data was set to 5 for Swedish and 2 for Chinese. These values were based on the number of documents we were using and our prior experience with English and Japanese.

4.1 Test data

For evaluating the English and Japanese systems there were obvious candidates for evaluation sets well-known to the QA community since the TREC and NTCIR QA evaluations have been running now for several years. For the English experiments we performed two sets of experiments using the TREC 2003 and TREC 2005 factoid QA questions. For the Japanese experiments we used the formal run of the NTCIR-3 QAC-1 task.

For Chinese and Swedish there were no such standard test sets available. We therefore decided to translate the first 200 questions in the TREC 2003 QA factoid task into Chinese and Swedish. For Swedish this was relatively straightforward. For Chinese, we didn't know the Chinese translation of the names, places etc. for about 40% of the original TREC questions. Such questions were therefore "translated" into a roughly equivalent question about something similar in China. However, the final set of Chinese questions still contained 17% of questions that had a U.S. background. Correct answers were found by a human to 91% and 93% of questions for Chinese and Swedish, respectively. We hope that using the TREC questions should at least give the reader some idea of the kind of the questions that were asked so they can appreciate the difficulty of finding the answers in Chinese and Swedish web data. To aid comprehension of the task we are tackling we have made the questions and the answers we used for evaluation freely available[2] for anyone else interested in running similar experiments.

4.2 Results

The TREC, NTCIR and CLEF QA evaluations have all converged on the use of exact and supported answers as a metric of QA system performance. In web-based QA we are also concerned with document support but primarily with answer correctness so for now we only use answer correctness as our evaluation metric. However, we also adopt the notion of inexact answers to mark as incorrect, answers that have extraneous or missing parts such as units of measurement or in the case of, say Chinese, an extra or missing character.

In Table 2 we present the number and percentage of answers that were marked correct in the top 1, 5, 10 and 20 answers output by each of the four monolingual systems.

[2] `http://asked.jp/About.html`

5 Discussion

Probably the first observation one makes looking at Table 2 is that the performance of the Chinese and Swedish systems is significantly lower than the English and Japanese systems. On the face of it this is not so surprising since far more documents and many more hours went into developing the English and Japanese systems for which the system parameters were also optimised on held-out question data prior to evaluation.

One significant issue common to our evaluation of the Chinese and Swedish systems is the use of a translation of the TREC 2003 questions. Although it was hoped this would aid comprehension of the task we were attempting it had the predictable problem that not enough, or any (in some cases), relevant Chinese and Swedish web data could be found to answer some questions. Particularly problematic were U.S. centric questions about baseball and U.S. geography of which there were around 5% and 10%, respectively, in the Swedish test set. However, aside from the choice of test data there are several other possible reasons for the drop in performance and we'll examine them separately for Chinese and Swedish in the following sections.

5.1 Chinese

One of the most important issues in building a Chinese QA system was deciding on the segmentation for text in which there are no spaces between words. In contrast to our Japanese system where we used a freely available segmentation tool we chose to segment Chinese text into single characters and to not even try to recover a notion of words from the text. Clearly this is far from satisfactory but the redundancy aspect of our approach does compensate for this to some extent by favouring frequent character sequences which are more likely to represent words. The second major problem we had was downloading sufficient and relevant data for each question. The largest culprit here was our restriction on using only 20 documents, the reasons for which were explained in Section 4. However, the quality of the documents themselves was also a problem: only 47.5% of questions had data in which the correct answer was observed at least once in the data and this was reduced to 43.5% when an answer had to occur 2 or more times. This places a much lower value on the performance upper bound (i.e. 47.5%) compared to English where it is typically 80-90% and consequently puts the results we obtained in a more positive light. Another interesting observation was that there were very few inexact answers (10% in the top 20) which shows that the modelling assumption made in Equation (5) was not detrimental for Chinese even when segmenting by characters.

5.2 Swedish

The general structure of Swedish and its character set are very similar to English so there were very few modifications that needed to be made to port the English system to Swedish. In some senses Swedish (and indeed many other European languages) are much easier than English for a purely statistical keyword-based system since they do not have the same phenomenon that English has where many[3] questions use *does/did* as in *"Who/when/where does/did ...?"* etc. questions. Swedish does, however, suffer from some of the same problems as English such as the need to re-order words in a question to produce a more statement-like formulation. A more significant problem is that Swedish is a language spoken by only about 9 million people and correspondingly there were far fewer training questions and answers freely available on the web and much less web-data available for finding answers. Although our maximum number of documents was set to 100, we only downloaded 48 documents per question on average (s.d. of 30). In a data-driven approach that relies to a large extent on data redundancy and the philosophy that "the more data the better" to achieve good performance this is always likely to be problematic. Indeed, of the documents that were downloaded for each question 67.5% contained a correct answer. This was reduced to 50% for correct answers occuring the threshold number of 5 times or more. Clearly a more linguistics-based system suffers less from this lack of redundancy but as pointed out earlier the problem is simply transferred to the development stage instead, where the initial data or linguistic knowledge needed to train a system might well be lacking.

6 Conclusion

In this paper we have shown that usable performance from two prototype QA systems developed

[3]For example, 28% of TREC 2003 factoid questions.

for Chinese and Swedish could be obtained in a matter of hours using our data-driven approach to question answering. While the performance of such systems was found to be below that of more developed systems that used the same approach we feel that this demonstrates the effectiveness of our language independent approach for web-based QA. One of the interesting observations from our experiments is the inherent difficulty of finding answers to questions when there is very little data available in the target language in which to search for answers. While one could argue that someone in Sweden or China may not be interested in finding out the winning team of the 1996 World Series this clearly misses the point and instead makes a compelling argument for cross-language QA (CLQA) whose profile has been steadily increasing due to the recent CLEF and NTCIR evaluations. While most attempts at CLQA have so far concentrated on translating the query into English and performing monolingual English QA on the translated query, we feel that an approach that also combines a simple system trained in the manner described in this paper would almost certainly benefit overall performance.

7 Further work

In the future we aim to improve the Chinese and Swedish systems by increasing the amount and quality of data used for training and also the data used for searching for answers as well as solving the explosion in memory usage that occurred with large amounts of Chinese text. We also intend to optimise the system parameters for each system using the questions and answers used for training with a rotating form of cross-validation so as to maximise use of the little data we have available. Given the rapid development time and reasonable performance of the approach outlined in this paper combined with the fact that specialized linguistic knowledge is unnecessary we also plan the development of yet more monolingual systems in other languages and hope to participate in the upcoming CLEF QA track.

8 Acknowledgments

This research was supported by JSPS and the Japanese government 21st century COE programme. The authors also with to thank Dietrich Klakow for his contributions to the model development.

References

E. Brill, S. Dumais, and M. Banko. 2002. An Analysis of the AskMSR Question-answering System. In *Proceedings of the 2002 Conference on Empirical Methods in Natural Language Processing (EMNLP)*.

M. Fuchigami, H. Ohnuma, and A. Ikeno. 2004. Oki QA System for QAC-2. In *Proceedings of NTCIR-4 Workshop*.

J. Fukumoto, T. Kato, and F. Masui. 2002. Question Answering Challenge (QAC-1) An Evaluation of Question Answering Task at NTCIR Workshop 3. In *Proceedings of NTCIR-3 Workshop*.

E. Hovy, U. Hermjakob, and Lin C-Y. 2001. The Use of External Knowledge in Factoid QA. In *Proceedings of the TREC 2001 Conference*.

S. M. Katz. 1987. Estimation of Probabilities from Sparse Data for the Language Model Component of a Speech Recognizer. *IEEE Transactions on Acoustic, Speech, and Signal Processing*, 35(3):400–401.

J. Lin, A. Fernandes, B. Katz, G. Marton, and S. Tellex. 2002. Extracting Answers from the Web Using Knowledge Annotation and Knowledge Mining Techniques. In *Proceedings of the Eleventh Text REtrieval Conference (TREC2002)*, Gaithersburg, Maryland, November.

D. Moldovan, S. Harabagiu, R. Girju, P. Morarescu, F. Lacatusu, A. Novischi, A. Badulescu, and O. Bolohan. 2002. LCC Tools for Question Answering. In *Proceedings of the TREC 2002 Conference*.

Willie Rogers. 2000. TREC Mandarin. Linguistic Data Consortium.

Sprakbanken Gothenburg University. 1997. PAROLE Swedish Language Corpus. `http://spraakbanken.gu.se/lbeng.html`.

E. Voorhees. 2002. Overview of the TREC 2002 Question Answering Track. In *Proceedings of the TREC 2002 Conference*.

E. Voorhees. 2003. Overview of the TREC 2003 Question Answering Track. In *Proceedings of the TREC 2003 Conference*.

E.W.D. Whittaker, P. Chatain, S. Furui, and D. Klakow. 2005a. TREC2005 Question Answering Experiments at Tokyo Institute of Technology. In *Proceedings of the 14th Text Retrieval Conference*.

E.W.D. Whittaker, S. Furui, and D. Klakow. 2005b. A Statistical Pattern Recognition Approach to Question Answering using Web Data. In *Proceedings of Cyberworlds*.

E.W.D. Whittaker, J. Hamonic, and S. Furui. 2005c. A Unified Approach to Japanese and English Question Answering. In *Proceedings of NTCIR-5*.

Dialogue based Question Answering System in Telugu

Rami Reddy Nandi Reddy
Dept. of Comp. Sc. & Engg,
Jadavpur University,
Kolkata, India
`nramireddy@gmail.com`

Sivaji Bandyopadhyay
Dept. of Comp. Sc. & Engg,
Jadavpur University,
Kolkata, India
`sivaji_cse_ju@yahoo.com`

Abstract

A dialogue based Question Answering (QA) system for Railway information in Telugu has been described. Telugu is an important language in India belonging to the Dravidian family. The main component of our QA system is the Dialogue Manager (DM), to handle the dialogues between user and system. It is necessary in generating dialogue for clarifying partially understood questions, resolving Anaphora and Co-reference problems. Besides, different modules have been developed for processing the query and its translation into formal database query language statement(s). Based on the result from the database, a natural language answer is generated. The empirical results obtained on the current system are encouraging. Testing with a set of questions in Railway domain, the QA system showed 96.34% of precision and 83.96% of dialogue success rate. Such a question answering system can be effectively utilized when integrated with a speech input and speech output system.

1 Introduction

Ever since Question Answering (QA) emerged as an active research field, the community has slowly diversified question types, increased question complexity, and refined evaluation metrics, as reflected by the TREC (Text Retrieval Conference) QA track (Voorhees, 2004). Several QA systems have responded to these changes in the nature of the QA task by incorporating various knowledge resources (Hovy et al., 2002), handling of additional types of questions tapping into external data sources such as web, encyclopedia, and databases in order to find the answer candidates, which may then be located in the specific corpus being searched (Xu et al., 2003).

The most popular classes of technique for QA are open-domain and restricted-domain (Diekema et al., 2004, Doan-Nguyen et al., 2004). These two domains use thesauri and lexicons in classifying documents and categorizing the questions. Open domain question answering deals with questions about nearly everything and can only rely on general ontology. It has become a very active research area over the past few years. On the other hand, Restricted-domain question answering (RDQA) deals with questions under a specific domain. If we create such a RDQA interface for structured e.g. relational database, we call it as Natural language interface to database system (NLIDB) (Androutsopoulos et al., 1995), where it allows the user to access the information stored in database by typing requests expressed in some natural language. RDQA has a long history, beginning with systems working over databases (e.g., BASEBALL (Green et al., 1961), and LUNAR (woods et al., 1972)).

In practice, current QAs can only understand limited subsets of natural language. Therefore, some training is still needed to teach the end-user what kinds of questions the system can or cannot understand. There are kinds of questions (e.g. questions involving negation, or quantification) that can be easily expressed in natural language, but that seem difficult (or at least tedious) to express using graphical or form based interfaces. Anaphoric and elliptical expressions are also handled by the QA systems. In recent years a large part of the research in QAs has been devoted to portability, i.e., to the design of QAs that can be used in different knowledge domains

(Knowledge domain portability), with different underlying Database Management System (DBMS) (DBMS portability), or even with different natural languages (Natural language portability). There is a growing body of research on integrating speech recognition, robust interpretation with the goal being to implement systems that engage users in spoken dialogue to help them perform certain tasks. We expect that this line of research will have a significant influence on future QAs, giving rise to systems that will allow users to access databases by spoken dialogue, in situations for which graphic and form-based interfaces are difficult to use.

A practical question answering system in restricted domain (Hoojung et al., 2004) and our system handles user questions similarly. However, our system extracts the information from a relational database. Moreover, our system keeps track of user dialogue and handles clarifications, elaborations and confirmations needed from the user with respect to the query. Along with it returns natural language answer in user-friendly format.

ARISE (Automatic Railway Information System for Europe) is a spoken dialogue system to provide train timetable information over the phone. Prototypes have been developed in four languages: Dutch, French, English, and Italian. ARISE uses a mixed initiative Dialogue Manager (DM). A mix of implicit and explicit confirmation is used, based on how confident the system is in deciding whether an item has been correctly understood.

We relate this paper as an experiment for designing a keyword based QA system for a huge domain (i.e. for Railways), which aims at replying users questions in their native language (Telugu). The system generates SQL query out of the natural language question, executes the SQL query over a relational database and then provide the answer. Dialogue Manager (DM) is maintained to generate dialogues with user and to handle the anaphoric and elliptical expression in our query. This system is implemented on a relatively restricted domain that includes a number of aspects of railway information system (Arrival/Departure time, Fare between for particular stations, Trains between important stations etc.). The precision of the information extraction stage is essential to the success of a QA system, because it places an upper bound on the precision of the entire system.

The empirical results obtained on the current system are encouraging. Testing with a set of questions in Railway domain, the QA system showed 96.34% of precision and 83.96% of dialogue success rate.

Section 2 deals with the System Architecture of the QA system. Section 3 details about the QA system design in the Railway information domain using the Keyword based approach. The evaluation has been carried out in Section 4. Section 5 concludes with some directions for future work.

2 System Architecture

In this keyword based approach the input query statement is analyzed by the query analyzer, which uses domain ontology stored as knowledge base, generating tokens and keywords. The appropriate query frame is selected based on the keywords and the tokens in the query statement. Each query frame is associated with a SQL generation procedure. The appropriate SQL statement(s) is generated using the tokens retrieved from the input query.

The QA system architecture is shown in Figure 1. The Dialogue Manager keeps track of the elliptical queries from the user that constitute the dialogue and helps in the SQL generation procedure using dialogue history (Flycht-Erikson et al., 2000), which contains information about previous tokens and their types as well as other dialogue information like answers retrieved by the current SQL statements and the answers for previous queries in the dialogue. The SQL statements used to retrieve the correct answer from the database. Based on the result of the DBMS, a natural language answer is generated. This answer is forwarded to the DM for onward transmission to the user.

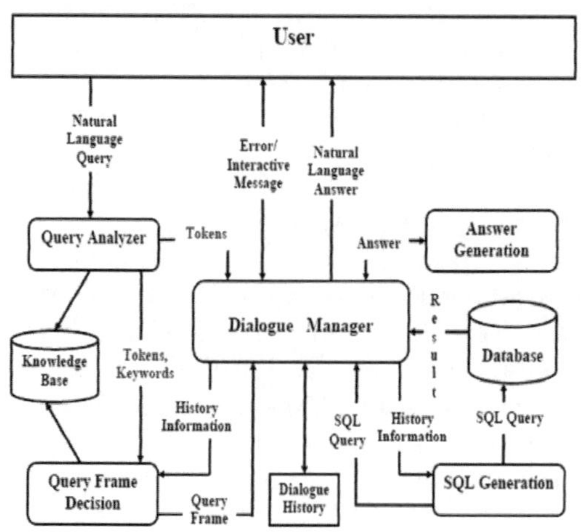

Figure 1. QA System Architecture

If the system cannot decide on the query frame by using the keywords extracted from the input query, the system enters into a dialogue with the user through the DM. During SQL generation if it is detected that more information is needed from the user to generate the SQL statement then an interactive message is sent to the user through the DM. The user will then send the needed information to the system. If user could not provide correct information then DM sends an error message to the user indicating the error in the user query. In case, the SQL statement generates a null response from the database the DM will send a cooperative message depending on the user query.

3 Design of Railway Information System

The most important issue in the design of the Railway information system is the design of the Railway database and the Knowledge base. These are detailed in Sections 3.1 & 3.2 respectively. The different components of the dialogue based QA system, i.e., Query Analyzer, Query Frame Decision, Dialogue Manager, SQL Generation and Answer Generation sub systems are described in subsequent sections.

3.1 Railway Database Management

The system as a whole is engaged in data access, and is a hybrid system with subsystem to analyze the natural language query and formal query language SQL, and a data retrieval and database management system. The *database* is structured and contains the information to provide the railway information service. For example in a Railway information system, database contains information about the arrival/departure time of trains, their fares and their running information etc. The aim of database management is to describe the information, in order to offer the service.

For our purposes the relational model has important advantage: The relational model stresses on data independence. This means that the user and front-end programs are effectively isolated from the actual database organization.

The main tables used here are schedule table for each train, fare tables for special trains like Rajdhani, Shatabdi etc. that have a different fare structure, Route tables for each route and tables that include train running frequency details etc. Some temporal tables are maintained in order to check the status of the railway ticket (which is known as checking the Passenger Name Record or PNR status of the ticket) and reservation availability information of a particular train.

3.2 Design of the Knowledge Base

The system maintains a knowledge base of the domain to facilitate question answering. For a system operating on a restricted domain this is quite obvious since it will greatly improve the disambiguation and parsing.

The words that occur in the database query for Railway information system includes words describing train name, station name, reservation class, and date and/or period of journey or keywords that specify the topic of the query. Hence we stored a domain dependent ontology in the knowledge base.

Knowledge base, which contains tables for train name, station name and alias tables for train name and station name. We have stored possible Telugu inflections (కి (*ke* [to]), కు (*ku* [to]), లో (*loo* [in]), తుంది (*tundi* [ing]), వి (*vi* [have]) etc. for ex: గుంటూరుకు (*gunturku* [to Guntur])), which can be used in *morphological analysis* of input query. We have considered possible postpositions like నుండి (*nundi* [from]), నుంచి (*nunchi* [from] etc. (For ex: న్యూఢిల్లీ నుండి (*newdelhi nundi* [from New Delhi])), which can be used to identify the source station in the input query and route words like దగ్గర (*daggara* [near]), ద్వారా (*dwara* [through]), గుండా (*gunda* [through]), వద్ద (*vadda* [at]), మీదుగా (*meedugaa* [via]) etc. (For ex: గయా మీదుగా (*gaya meedugaa* [via Gaya])), which can be used to identify the route station of the journey. We kept a list of keywords in a table in order to identify the proper query frame.

3.3 Query Analyzer

During query analysis, Morphological analysis of the input query statement is carried out to identify the root words / terms. Analyzing the whole input query, the system identifies several tokens such as Train name, Station name, Reservation class, date and period of the day etc. and a set of keywords.

The query analyzer consults the domain-dependent ontology i.e. knowledge base for recognizing these tokens and keywords. It may happen that some words/terms may not found in the knowledge base. Those words do not contain any semantic information and are simply discarded.

For example: If our input query is ఎప్పుడు ఫలక్ నుమా ఎక్స్‌ప్రెస్ గుంటూరుకు వెళ్తుంది (*eppudu falaknuma express gunturuku veltundi* [When the Falaknuma Express goes to Guntur])

Here query is parsed based on spaces. After parsing each word, it is searched in the knowledge base until the word is found. After searching each word/term in the knowledge base, their types and semantic information are put in a list of tokens. Each token has three properties: the token value, its type and semantic information that it contains. These tokens and keywords are used to decide the proper query frame.

For the above example, the tokens identified are ఫలక్ నుమా ఎక్స్‌ప్రెస్ (Falaknuma Express) as Train name and గుంటూరు (Guntur) as Station name. Whereas ఎప్పుడు (*eppudu* [when]), వెళ్తుంది (*veltundi* [goes]) are under keywords list.

3.4 Query Frame Decision

During the analysis of query, the keywords in the input query are detected. In this step, based on the tokens and keywords, we identify the appropriate *query frame.*

Restricting the query domain and information resource, the scope of the user request can be focused. That is, there are a finite number of expected question topics. Each expected question topic is defined under a single query frame. Some query frame examples for Railway information system are fare of a journey [Fare], arrival [Arr_Time] or departure time [Dep_Time] of a train, trains between important stations [Trains_Imp_Stations], scheduled time [Sched_Time], weekly frequency of a train [Arr_Frequency / Dep_Frequency], Availability of reservation class in a particular train [Reservation_Availability] and PNR enquiry [PNR_Enquiry].

It is important to select the appropriate query frame for the user request; because in some cases ambiguity will occur i.e. a single natural language query statement may belong to one or more query frames means same keywords are used to identify the query frames.

For example keywords like వెళ్ళు (*vellu* [*go*]), వచ్చు (*vachhu* [come]), చేరు (*cheru* [reach]), and బయలుదేరు (*bayuluderu* [start]) etc. are used to identify the query frames [Arr_Time], [Dep_Time], and [Trains_Imp_Stations]. To resolve this ambiguity, we consider what/which (question having words ఏ (*ee* [what]), ఏఏ (*eeee* [what]), ఏవి (*evi* [which]) etc.) type of questions like న్యూఢిల్లీ నుండి హౌరాకు బయలుదేరు రైళ్ళు ఏవి (*newdelhi nundi howrahku bayaluderu raillu evi* [What are the trains starts from New Delhi to Howrah]) are under [Trains_Imp_Stations] query frame. Where as, when (questions having words ఎప్పుడు (*eppudu* [when]), ఎన్నిగంటలకు (*ennigantalaku* [at what time]), ఎన్నింటికి (*ennintiki* [at what time]) etc.) type of questions like ఎన్నిగంటలకు కోల్కతా రాజధాని ఎక్స్‌ప్రెస్ బయలుదేరుతుంది (*ennigantalaku kolkata rajadhani express bayaluderutundi* [When Kolkata Rajdhani Express starts]) are under [Dep_Time] query frame. Similarly, weekday names like సోమవారము (*somavaaramu*) [Monday], మంగళవారము (*mangalavaaramu*) [Tuesday] etc. and keywords used in [Arr_Time]/ [Dep_Time] query frame are used to identify the [Arr_Frequency]/ [Dep_Frequency] query frame.

In contrast, separate keywords are used to identify [Arr_Time] and [Dep_Time] query frames. But keywords like పోతుంది (*potundi* [go]), వెళ్ళు (*vellu* [go]) etc. are used to identify both [Arr_Time] and [Dep_Time] query frames. To resolve this ambiguity, we consider the station type, i.e. whether the station is source or destination. If the station is source station (station name succeeded by postpositions like నుండి (*nundi* [from]), నుంచి (*nunchi* [from])), then we conclude that our query is under [Dep_Time] query frame. Otherwise query will be under [Arr_Time] query frame. For example, questions like ఎప్పుడు ఫలక్ నుమా ఎక్స్‌ప్రెస్ గుంటూరుకు వెళ్తుంది (*eppudu falaknuma express gunturuku veltundi* [When the Falaknuma Express goes to Guntur]) is under [Arr_Time] query frame. But, questions like ఎప్పుడు ఫలక్ నుమా ఎక్స్‌ప్రెస్ గుంటూరు నుండి వెళ్తుంది (*eppudu falaknuma express gunturu nundi veltundi* [When the Falaknuma Express goes from Guntur]) is under [Dep_Time] query frame.

The selection process of query frame has a great influence on the precision of the system, while there is not much likelihood of errors in other processes, such as getting the information from the dialogue history or generating SQL statement(s) from the selected query frame and/or retrieving the answer from the database and generating natural language answer from the retrieved result.

3.5 Dialogue Manager

The role of the Dialogue Manager (DM) differs slightly between different dialogue systems. But the primary responsibility of the DM is to control the flow of dialogue by deciding how the system should respond to a user request and the coordination of the other components in the system. If some information is missing or a request is ambiguous, clarification questions are specified by the DM and posed to the user.

For example in general, users ask questions about Arrival/Departure time without mentioning journey of train i.e. Upward/Downward journey, then system asks the user for proper information. Sometimes user may not give correct information (like missing Train name, Station name or query does not belong to any of the query frames etc.). At that time DM generates error message describing that missed information. In another case user asks questions without knowledge. In this case DM generates a *cooperative message,* which will help the user in further requests.

As a basis for the above tasks the DM utilizes the *dialogue history*. Here dialogue history records the focal information, i.e what has been talked in the past and what is talking at present. It is used for dialogue control and disambiguation of context dependent requests. The DM gets a semantic frame from the other system components. This frame is filled by interpreting the request in the context of the ongoing dialogue, domain knowledge, and dialogue history. The DM then prompts for missing information or sends a SQL query. Before the query is sent off, DM checks whether new information is contained in the query or the information is contradictory to information given before. If this is the case then the DM can either keep the original information or replace it with the new one in the dialogue history or engage in a confirmation subdialogue.

The DM looks at the query after language processing has been completed (but before the formal query is issued), as well as after the result has been obtained from the formal query. The accuracy of the system mainly depends on the representation of the dialogue history and how the DM responds to the user's dialogue.

3.6 SQL Generation

Once the query frame is selected for a question, the corresponding procedure for the SQL query generation is called. For each query frame there is a procedure for SQL statement(s) generation. In order to generate the SQL query, it needs the tokens generated by the query analyzer.

If the tokens are presented in the current query, it uses them. Otherwise it gets the token information from the dialogue history. For example, in the arrival time queries user has to specify Train name/no and station/city name where he/she needs to go. If he/she did not mention that information, SQL generation procedure gets the information from the dialogue history. Figure 2 depicts the conversion of natural language query to its SQL query.

ఎప్పుడు ఫలక్‌నుమా ఎక్స్‌ప్రెస్ గుంటూరుకు వెళ్తుంది (eppudu falaknuma express gunturuku veltundi When the Falaknuma Express goes to Guntur])?

↓

Train name: ఫలక్‌నుమా ఎక్స్‌ప్రెస్ (Falaknuma Express)
Station name: గుంటూరు (Guntur)
Keywords: ఎప్పుడు (e*ppudu* [when]), వెళ్తుంది (*veltundi* [goes]).

↓

The [Arr_Time] Query frame is selected.

↓

The system checks with the user for up/down journey of the train

↓

Let user asked about upward journey of train via DM.

↓

SELECT Arr_Time FROM Schedule2703 WHERE Station Name='గుంటూరు'.

Figure 2: Interpreting the natural language question to the SQL query

For the fare related query, SQL generation procedure would be called depending on the type of train. The procedure considers that the user will provide the train name and reservation class. If the train is of Express type, it considers that the user may provide either the source and destination stations of journey or the distance of journey. If it is of Rajdhani type, it considers that the user may provide source and destination station of journey. Similarly for the other query frames, SQL generation procedure considers that the user provide the necessary information.

3.7 Answer Generation

Once the SQL statement for an input query statement is generated, it is triggered on the database and the retrieved information is used to represent the answer. The retrieved information is updated in the dialogue history for further reference.

SELECT Arr_Time FROM Schedule2703 WHERE Station_Name='గుంటూరు'.

↓

DBMS returns "04:33 hrs".

↓

4:33 గంటలకు ఫలక్‌నుమా ఎక్స్‌ప్రెస్ గుంటూరుకు వెళ్తుంది (*04:33 gantalaku falaknuma express gunturku veltundi* [At 04:33hrs Falaknuma Express goes to Guntur]).

Figure 3: Generating answer from the retrieved result.

Each query frame has its corresponding Answer generator. We use template based answer generation method. Each template consists of several slots. Those slots are filled by the retrieved answer and the tokens generated from the query. Figure 3 shows the answer generation from the SQL query generated from the natural language query shown in Figure 2. The answer will be sent to Dialogue Manager, which will further send it to the user.

4 Evaluation

For evaluating our system we have taken queries from our Telugu-speaking friends. We have described the Railway Information system to them. They have also been told about the constraints on the nature of queries in the systems. They have also been shown list of example queries for the systems.

Here we are considering two measures for evaluating our system: *Dialogue success rate* and *Precision.* The QA system was evaluated by giving 26 sets of dialogue consisting 95 natural language queries in total. The two evaluation measures are defined as follows:

Dialogue success rate for each set=Number of Answers or Responses generated by the system /Number of turns issued by the user.

Dialogue success rate = ($\sum$ Dialogue success rate for each set / Number of sets of dialogues)*100.

Precision= (Number of correct answers given by the system/Number of answers given by the system)*100.

The number of turns issued by the user in a dialogue is the total of the number of questions issued to the system and the number of responses provided by the user to the system.

Each set of dialogue consisted of around 3 to 5 natural language queries. The total dialogue success rate for the 26 sets was obtained as 21.83. The dialogue success rate for the system is calculated as

Dialogue success rate= (21.83/26)*100= 83.96%.

Out of 95 questions, system generated answers for 82 questions of which 79 were correct answers. So, the precision of the system is calculated as

Precision= (79/82)*100= 96.34%.

This low dialogue success rate is due to the fact that the system coverage of the domain is not extensive enough, i.e., query frames for some natural language queries were not correctly identified. The information given by the user in the query was sometimes inadequate and the system was not able to identify the missing information because of the incorrect choice of the query frame. Sometimes the system is unable to obtain tokens correctly from the input query even if it had identified the right query frame, thereby generating wrong answers. Misinterpretation of dialogue history is also another problem.

5 Conclusion

In this dialogue based QA system following the keyword based approach, each word need not be found in the knowledge base. Only the words that contain semantic information needs to be found in the knowledge base.

By restricting the coverage of questions, our system could achieve relatively high dialogue success rate. However, for a real practical system this success rate must be improved.

In extension to our work we are developing the modules for the remaining query frames. The system needs to be upgraded so that a user can query for railway information over phone. The speech input can be converted to textual query. This textual query can be input of our system and the textual out can be converted to speech again to answer the user.

References

Androutsopoulos I, Ritchie G. D, and Thanisch P. 1995. Natural Language Interfaces to Databases –

An Introduction. *Natural Language Engineering*, Vol 1, Part1, 29–81.

Diekema A.R, Yilmazel Ozgur, and Liddy E.D. 2004. Evaluation of Restricted Domain Question-Answering Systems. In *Proceedings of the ACL2004 Workshop on Question Answering in Restricted Domain*, 2-7.

Doan-Nguyen Hai and Leila Kosseim. 2004. The Problem of Precision in Restricted-Domain Question Answering. Some Proposed Methods of Improvement. In *Proceedings of the ACL 2004 Workshop on Question Answering in Restricted Domain*, 8-15.

Flycht-Eriksson Annika and Jonsson Arne. 2000 Dialogue and Domain Knowledge Management in Dialogue Systems. In *proceedings of 1st SIGDIAL workshop at ACL2000.*

Green W, Chomsky C, and Laugherty K. 1961. BASEBALL: An automatic question answerer. *Proceedings of the Western Joint Computer Conference*, 219-224.

Hoojung Chung, Young-In Song, Kyoung-Soo Han, Do-Sang Yoon, Joo-Young Lee, Hae-Chang Rim and Soo-Hong Kim. 2004. A Practical QA System in Restricted Domains. In *Proceedings of the ACL 2004 Workshop on Question Answering in Restricted Domain*, 39-45.

Hovy E, Hermjakob U, Lin C.Y, and Ravichnadran D. 2002. Using knowledge to facilitate factoid answer pinpointing .*COLING*.

Voorhees E.M. 2004. Overview of the TREC 2003 question answering track. In *Proceedings of the 12th Text REtrieval Conference*.

Woods W.A, Kaplan R.M, and Webber B.N.1972 The Lunar Sciences Natural Language Information System: Final Report. BBN Report 2378, *Bolt Beranek and Newman Inc.*, Cambridge, Massachusetts.

Xu J, Licuanan A and Weischedel R. 2003. TREC 2003 qa at bbn: Answering definitional questions. *TREC.*

Appendix: Examples of QA in the system

Example 1:
U: ఎన్నిగంటలకు కోల్‌కతా రాజధాని ఎక్స్‌ప్రస్ బయలుదేరుతుంది (*ennigantalaku kolkata rajadhani express bayaluderutundi* [When Kolkata Rajdhani Express starts])?
S: పైకా(*pikaa* [is it up])/క్రిందికా (*krindikaa* [is it down])
U: పైకు (*piku* [up])
S: 16:15 గంటలకు కోల్‌కతా రాజధాని ఎక్స్‌ప్రస్ హౌరా నుండి బయలుదేరుతుంది (*16:15 gantalaku kolkata rajadhani express howrah nundi bayaluderutundi* [At 16:15hrs Kolkata Rajdhani Express starts from Howrah]).

Example 2:
U: కోల్‌కతా రాజధాని ఎక్స్‌ప్రస్‌లో ఫస్ట్ ఎసికు టుటైర్ ఎసికు హౌరా నుండి మొఘల్‌సరాయ్‌కి టిక్కెట్టు ధర ఎంత
(*Kolkata rajadhani expressloo first acku twotier acku howrah nundi mughulsaraike tikkettu dhara enta* [What is the fare between Howrah to Mughalsarai in Kolkata Rajdhani Express for First A.C, Two Tier A.C])?
S: కోల్‌కతా రాజధాని ఎక్స్‌ప్రస్‌లో ఫస్ట్ ఎసికు టుటైర్ ఎసికు హౌరా నుండి మొఘల్‌సరాయ్‌కి టిక్కెట్టు ధర 2061, 1060 రూపాయిలు. (*Kolkata rajadhani expressloo first acku twotier acku howrah nundi mughulsaraike tikeettu dhara 2061, 1060 rupaayulu* [Fare from Howrah to Mughulsarai in Kolkata Rajdhani Express for First A.C, Two Tier A.C is 2061, 1060 respectively]).
U: స్లీపర్ క్లాస్‌కు (*sleeper classku* [to Sleeper Class]
(Here it refers to the previous request of the user)
S: కోల్‌కతా రాజధాని ఎక్స్‌ప్రస్‌లో ఫస్ట్ ఎసి, టుటైర్ ఎసి , త్రీటైర్ ఎసి మాత్రమే ఉంటాయి. (*kolkata rajadhani expressloo first ac, twotier ac, three tier ac matramee untayi* [Rajdhani Express has First AC, Two Tier AC and Three Tier AC only]). Because in India, Rajdhani Express won't has Sleeper Class. This cooperative message generated by the DM.

Example 3:
U: సికింద్రాబాద్ నుండి తిరుపతికు ఏఏ రైళ్ళు ఉన్నాయి (*secundrabad nundi tirupatiki eeee raillu unnayi* [What are the trains from Secunderabad to Tirupati])?
S: కృష్ణా ఎక్స్‌ప్రస్ (Krishna Express),శబరి ఎక్స్‌ప్రస్ (Sabari Express), పద్మావతి ఎక్స్‌ప్రస్ (Padmavati Express), నారాయణాద్రి ఎక్స్‌ప్రస్ (Narayanadri Express).
U: ఏవి సోమవారము బయలుదేరుతాయి (*evi somavaaramu bayaluderutayi* [Which start on Monday])?
S: కృష్ణా ఎక్స్‌ప్రస్ (Krishna Express),శబరి ఎక్స్‌ప్రస్ (Sabari Express), నారాయణాద్రి ఎక్స్‌ప్రస్ (Narayanadri Express).
U: ఎన్నింటికి నారాయణాద్రి ఎక్స్‌ప్రస్ వెళ్తుంది (*ennintiki narayanadri express veltundi* [When Narayanadri Express goes])?

S: 07:15 గంటలకు నారాయణాద్రి ఎక్స్‌ప్రెస్ తిరుపతి వెళ్తుంది (*07:15 gantalaku narayanadri express tirupati veltundi* [At 07:15 hrs Narayanadri Express goes to Tirupati]).

Example 4:
U: సికింద్రాబాద్ నుండి తిరుపతికు ఏ రైళ్ళు వెళ్తాయి (*secundrabad nundi tirupatiki ee raillu veltayi* [What are the trains from Secunderabad to Tirupati])?
S: కృష్ణా ఎక్స్‌ప్రెస్ (Krishna Express),శబరి ఎక్స్‌ప్రెస్ (Sabari Express), పద్మావతి ఎక్స్‌ప్రెస్ (Padmavati Express), నారాయణాద్రి ఎక్స్‌ప్రెస్ (Narayanadri Express).
U: ఏది త్వరగా వెళ్తుంది (*edi twaragaa veltundi* [Which Goes Early])?
S: No answer. Because keyword త్వరగా (*twaragaa* [early]) was not found in the knowledge base.i.e query belongs to another query frame.

Adapting a Semantic Question Answering System to the Web

Sven Hartrumpf
Intelligent Information and Communication Systems (IICS)
University of Hagen (FernUniversität in Hagen)
58084 Hagen, Germany
Sven.Hartrumpf@fernuni-hagen.de

Abstract

This paper describes how a question answering (QA) system developed for small-sized document collections of several million sentences was modified in order to work with a monolingual subset of the web. The basic QA system relies on complete sentence parsing, inferences, and semantic representation matching. The extensions and modifications needed for useful and quick answers from web documents are discussed. The main extension is a two-level approach that first accesses a web search engine and downloads some of its document hits and then works similar to the basic QA system. Most modifications are restrictions like a maximal number of documents and a maximal length of investigated document parts; they ensure acceptable answer times. The resulting web QA system is evaluated on the German test collection from QA@CLEF 2004. Several parameter settings and strategies for accessing the web search engine are investigated. The main results are: precision-oriented extensions and experimentally derived parameter settings are needed to achieve similar performance on the web as on small-sized document collections that show higher homogeneity and quality of the contained texts; adapting a semantic QA system to the web is feasible, but answering a question is still expensive in terms of bandwidth and CPU time.

1 Introduction

There are question answering (QA) systems intended for small-sized document collections (*textual QA systems*) and QA systems aiming at the web (*web(-based) QA systems*). In this paper, a system of the former type (InSicht, see (Hartrumpf, 2005b)) is transformed into one of the latter type (called InSicht-W3 for short). In Sect. 2, the textual QA system for German is presented. The extensions and modifications required to get it working with the web as a virtual document collection are described and discussed in Sect. 3. The resulting system is evaluated on a well-known test collection and compared to the basic QA system (Sect. 4). After the conclusion, some directions for further research are indicated.

2 The Basic QA System

The semantic[1] QA system that was turned into a web QA system is InSicht. It relies on complete sentence parsing, inferences, and semantic representation matching and comprises six main steps.

In the *document processing* step, all documents from a given collection are transformed into a standard XML format (CES, corpus encoding standard, see http://www.cs.vassar.edu/CES/) with word, sentence, and paragraph borders marked up by XML elements *w*, *s*, and *p*, respectively. Then, all preprocessed documents are parsed by WOCADI (Hartrumpf, 2003) yielding a syntactic dependency structure and, more importantly, a semantic representation, a semantic network of the MultiNet formalism (Helbig, 2006) for each document sentence. The parser can produce intersentential coreference links for a document.

In the second step (*query processing*), the user's question is parsed by WOCADI. Determining the sentence type (here, often a subtype of *question*) is especially important because it controls some parts of two later steps: query expansion and answer generation.

Next comes *query expansion*: Equivalent and similar semantic networks are derived from the original query network by means of lexico-

[1] *Semantic* in the sense that formal semantic representations of documents and questions are automatically produced by a parser and form the system center.

semantic relations from HaGenLex (Hagen German Lexicon, (Hartrumpf et al., 2003)) and a lexical database (GermaNet), equivalence rules, and inferential rules like entailments for situations (applied in backward chaining). The result is a set of disjunctively connected semantic networks that try to cover many possible kinds of representations of sentences possibly containing an explicit or implicit answer to the user's question.

In the fourth step (*semantic network matching*), all document sentences matching at least one of the semantic networks from query expansion are collected. A two-level approach is chosen for efficiency reasons. First, an index of concepts (disambiguated words with IDs from the lexicon) is consulted with the relevant concepts from the query networks. Second, the retrieved documents are compared sentence network by sentence network to find a match with a query network.

Answer generation is next: Natural language (NL) generation rules are applied to semantic networks that match a query network in order to generate an NL answer string from the deep semantic representations. The sentence type and the semantic network control the selection of generation rules. The rules also act as a filter for uninformative or bad answers. The results are tuples of generated answer string, numerical score, supporting document ID, and supporting sentence ID.

To deal with different answer candidates, an *answer selection* step is required. It realizes a quite simple but successful strategy that combines a preference for more frequent answers and a preference for more elaborate answers. The best answers (by default only the single best answer) and the supporting sentences are presented to the user that posed the question.

The first step, document processing, is run offline in InSicht; it is run online in InSicht-W3 to avoid unacceptable parsing costs before the system can be used. The remaining five steps will be left mostly unchanged for InSicht-W3, in parts just differently parameterized.

3 QA System Extensions for the Web

3.1 A Naive Approach to Web-based QA

The simplest approach to turning InSicht into a web QA system would be to collect German web pages and work with the resulting document collection as described in Sect. 2. However, a deep semantic analyzer will need several years to parse all web pages in German (even if excluding the pages from the much larger *deep web*). The following formula provides a rough estimate[2] of the CPU years needed:

$$\begin{aligned} t &= \frac{\text{\#documents} \cdot \text{\#sent\_per\_document}\,[sent]}{\text{parser\_speed}\,[sent/h]} \\ &= \frac{500{,}000{,}000 \cdot 320\,[sent]}{4000\,[sent/h]} \\ &= 40{,}000{,}000\,h \quad \approx \quad 4{,}566\,a \end{aligned}$$

This long time indicates that the naive approach is currently not an option. Therefore a multi-level approach was investigated. In this paper, only a two-level approach is discussed, which has been tried in shallow QA systems.

3.2 A Two-Level Approach to Web-based QA

As in other applications, a web search engine can be used (as a first level) to preselect possibly relevant documents for the task at hand (here, answering a question posed by a user). In InSicht-W3, the web is accessed when similar and equivalent semantic networks have been generated during query expansion. Clearly, one cannot directly use this semantic representation for retrieving document URLs from any service out there on the web—at least till the arrival of a web annotated with formal NL semantics. One must transform the semantic networks to an adequate level; in many web search engines, this is the level of search terms connected in a Boolean formula using *and* and *or*.

To derive a search engine query from a semantic network, all *lexical concepts* from the semantic network are collected. For example, question qa04_068 from QA@CLEF 2004 in example (1) leads to the semantic network depicted in Fig. 1 (and related semantic networks; for a QA@CLEF 2004 question, 4.8 additional semantic networks on average).

(1) Wo sitzt Hugo Lacour hinter Gittern?
Where sits Hugo Lacour behind bars?
'Where is Hugo Lacour imprisoned?'

The lexical concepts are roughly speaking those concepts (represented as nodes in graphical form) whose names are not of the form *c1*, *c2*, etc. The lexical concepts are named after the lemma of the

[2]The average number of sentences per document has been determined from a sample of 23,800 preprocessed web documents in InSicht-W3.

Figure 1: Semantic network for CLEF question qa04_068: *Wo sitzt Hugo Lacour hinter Gittern?* (*'Where is Hugo Lacour imprisoned?'*). Some edges are shown folded below the node name.

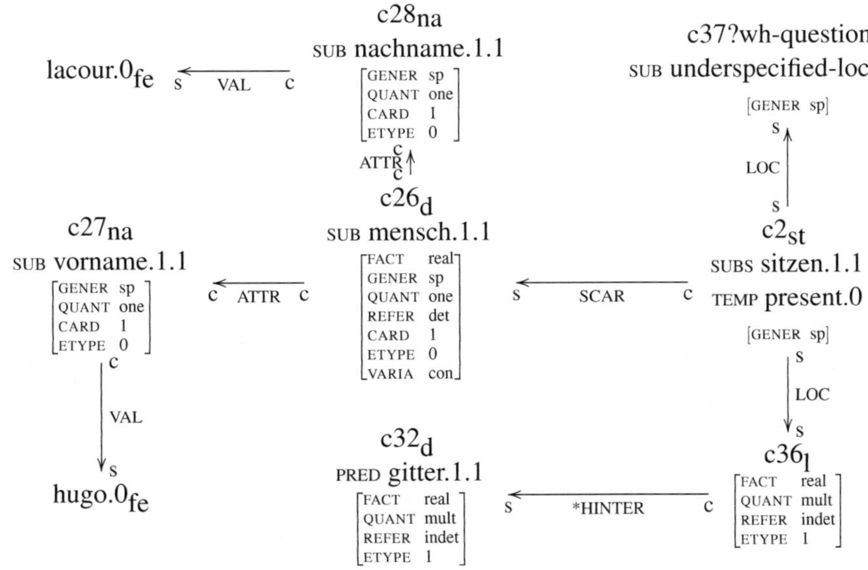

corresponding word plus a numerical homograph identifier and a numerical reading identifier.

As current web search engines provide no (or only rough) lemmatization for German, one must go one step further away from the semantic network by generating full forms for each word belonging to a lexical concept. (Others have tried a similar approach; for example, Neumann and Sacaleanu (2005) construct IR queries which can be easily adapted to different IR engines.) In the example, the node *sitzen.1.1* (*to sit*) leads to 26 different full forms (shown below in example (2)). These forms can be used as search terms; as alternatives, they are connected disjunctively. Thus for each semantic network from query expansion, a conjunction of disjunctions of word forms is constructed. Word forms can belong to words not occurring in the question because query expansion can introduce new concepts (and thereby new words), e.g. by inferential rules. The Boolean formulae for several semantic networks are connected disjunctively and the resulting formula is simplified by applying logical equivalences. What one can pass to a web search engine as a *preselection query* for question (1) is shown in prefix notation in example (2):

(2) *(or*
(and
(or *Gitter Gittern Gitters*)
(or *Hugo Hugos*)
(or *Lacour Lacours*)
(or gesessen gesessene gesessenem gesessenen gesessener gesessenes saß saßen saßest saßet saßt sitze sitzen sitzend sitzende sitzendem sitzenden sitzender sitzendes sitzest sitzet sitzt säße säßen säßest säßet))
. . . ; query derived from second query network
)

If a search engine does not offer Boolean operators (or limits Boolean queries to some hundred characters), one can transform the Boolean query into DNF and issue for each disjunct a search engine query that requires all its terms (for example, by prepending a plus sign to every term).

There are several problems related to breaking down a semantic network representation into a Boolean formula over word forms. For example, lexical concepts that do not stem from a surface form in the question should be excluded from the query. An example is the concept *nachname.1.1* (*'last name'*) which the named entity subparser of WOCADI installs in the semantic network when constructing the semantic representation of a human being whose last name is specified in the text (see Fig. 1).

The generation of a preselection query described above indicates that there is a fundamental *level mismatch* between the first level (web search engine) and the second level (an NL understanding system like the QA system InSicht): words (plus proximity information[3]) vs. concepts within (possibly normalized) semantic representations of sentences (or texts). This level mismatch deteriorates the precision of the first level and thereby the recall of the second level. The latter might be surprising. The precision of the first level (viewed in isolation) is not problematic because the second level achieves the same precision no matter how low the precision of the first level is. But precision *does* matter because the limited number of documents that the first level can return and that the second level can efficiently process might lead to not seeing relevant documents (i.e. lower recall) or at least to seeing them much later (which can imply unacceptable answer times). Or to put it differently: Very low precision in the first level can lead to lower recall of the whole multi-level system if there are any retrieval set limits for the first level.

At the end of the first level, the retrieved web documents are simplified by a script that uses the text dump function of the *lynx* web browser to extract the textual content. The resulting document representations can be processed by InSicht.

3.3 Deficiencies of Web Search Engines

Web search engines typically restrict the length of queries, e.g. to 1000 bytes, 1500 bytes, or 10 terms. But the rich morphology of languages like German can lead to long and complex preselection queries so that one needs to reduce preselection queries as far as possible (e.g. by dropping rare word forms). An additional strategy is to split the query into several independent subqueries.

The QA system is currently based on matching semantic representations with the granularity of a sentence only. Thus one would achieve much better precision if the web search engine allowed a *same-sentence* operator or at least a proximity operator (often named *NEAR*) of say 50 words which ignores linguistic units like sentences and paragraphs but suffices for our goals. Although some web search engines once had some kind of proximity operator, currently none of the search engines with large indices and Boolean queries seems to offer this facility.

3.4 Pragmatic Limits for Web-based QA

Pragmatic limits are needed to ensure acceptable answer times when dealing with the vast number of web documents. The following constraining parameters are implemented in InSicht-W3:

number of documents d **(BT-R)** [4] The number of documents retrieved from a search engine is limited by InSicht-W3. A separate query is sent to the search engine for each top-level disjunct, which corresponds to one semantic network. For each of the q subqueries, d/q documents are retrieved, at most.

Many search engines employ a maximal number of hits h. (A popular choice is currently 1000.) Due to other filtering constraints (like snippet testing as defined below), the limit h can inhibit the performance of InSicht-W3 even if h is greater than d.

document format (BT-R) Only documents encoded as HTML or plain text are covered. Other formats are omitted by adding a format constraint to the preselection query, by investigating the URL, and by interpreting the result of the UNIX program *file*.

document language (BPT-R) Only documents that are mainly written in German are treated. A language identification module is available in InSicht-W3, but the selection of document language in the web search engine was precise enough.

document length l **(T-R)** If a document is longer than l bytes it is shortened to the first l bytes (current value: 1,000,000 bytes).

document URL (BPT-R) The URL of a document must belong to certain top-level domains (.at, .ch, .de, .info, .net, .org) and must not be on a blacklist. Both conditions aim at higher quality pages. The blacklist is short and should be replaced by one that is collaboratively maintained on the web.

snippet testing (BPT-R) Many search engines return a *text snippet* for each search hit that typically contains all word forms from the search engine query. Sometimes the snippet does not fulfill the preselection query. A stronger constraint is that a snippet passage

[3] At least some years ago and hopefully in the future again, see Sect. 3.3.

[4] Trade-offs (and goals) are indicated in parentheses, between bandwidth (B), precision (P), (answer) time (T), on the one hand, and recall (R), on the other hand.

without ellipsis (...) must fulfill the preselection query. This realizes an imperfect *same-sentence* or similar proximity operator.

word form selection (BT-R) To shorten preselection queries for highly inflecting word categories (e.g. German verbs), InSicht-W3 omits full forms that are less likely to be contained in answering document sentences (e.g. verb forms that can only be imperative or first and second person). For adjectives, only the forms matching the degree (positive, comparative, and superlative in German) used in the question are included. The most restrictive parameter setting is to choose only one word form per content word, e.g. the word form occurring in the question.

These constraints can be checked before the second level starts.

The following parameters are applicable on the second level:

number of parsed sentences s **(T-R)** For each document, at most s sentences are parsed (current value: 100).

sentence language (PT-R) As many web pages contain passages in several languages, it is sometimes important to discard sentences that seem to be in a different language than the document itself. If the percentage of unknown words in a sentences reaches a threshold, the sentence is considered to be written in a foreign language

sentence selection (T) Only a sentence whose set of word forms fulfills the preselection query sent to the web search engine is parsed by WOCADI. This realizes a *same-sentence* operator on the second level. Of course, this operator would be more helpful in the web search engine (see Sect. 3.3).

3.5 Parameter Settings of the QA System

In general, the QA system must be parameterized differently when going from a high quality, low-redundancy, small-sized collection (like archives of some newspapers) to a mixed quality, high-redundancy, large-sized collection (like a considerable subset of the web). For example, the variation of concepts (like synonyms, hyponyms, and hyperonyms) is less important on the web than in smaller collections due to its large redundancy and increased chance to find a formulation whose semantic representation contains exactly the concepts from the question. This is helpful because full concept variations lead for some questions to very long preselection queries.

3.6 Language-specific Problems

InSicht-W3 has to deal with several problems in the German language and German web pages, which might be less problematic for English or some other languages. On the one hand, the rich morphology requires to generate word forms for content words derived from query networks; on the other hand, to avoid very long preselection queries the generation must be limited (e.g. with the word form selection parameter).

The morphological phenomenon of separable prefix verbs in German requires special treatment. Certain word forms of such verbs must appear as one orthographic word or two orthographic words (often separated by many intervening words). The choice depends on the word order of the sentence or clause that contains the verb. InSicht-W3's preselection queries contain both variants, e.g. for the word form *absitzt* the following formula is generated: *(or absitzt (and ab sitzt))*.

In German web pages, two orthography systems can be found, the old one and the new one introduced in 1998. As both systems are often mixed in pages (and question sets), the NL parsing must be flexible and exploit the links between old spellings, new spellings, and spelling variants. The parser normalizes all words and concept names to the old orthography. For preselection queries, word forms for all orthography systems must be generated.

Not only the orthography system might change in a web page, also the language itself might switch (often without correct markup), e.g. between English and German. Therefore the sentence language parameter from Sect. 3.4 was introduced. Such effects also occur for other languages.

German texts contain important characters that are not covered by the ASCII character set. (The most frequent ones are *ä*, *ö*, *ü*, *Ä*, *Ö*, *Ü*, and *ß*.) Unfortunately, different character encodings are used for German web pages, sometimes with a mismatch of declared (or implied) encoding and actually used encoding. This problem has been successfully delegated to the *lynx* web browser (see end of Sect. 3.2).

Table 1: Evaluation results for the German questions from QA@CLEF 2004. InSicht used all 200 questions, InSicht-W3 only 170 questions (see text).

setup		answers (%)					K1
system	document collection	non-empty			empty		
		right	inexact	wrong	right	wrong	
InSicht	QA@CLEF document collection	30.5	2.5	0.0	10.0	57.0	0.28
InSicht-W3	web (as virtual document collection)	22.9	2.9	2.4	0.0	71.8	0.18

4 Evaluation of the Web QA System

The resulting web QA system is evaluated on an established set of test questions: QA@CLEF 2004 (Magnini et al., 2005). Some questions in this set have an important implicit temporal context. For example, the correct answer to questions like qa04_090 in example (3) critically depends on the time this present tense question is uttered.

(3) Wer ist Präsident von UNICE?
Who is president of UNICE?

In QA@CLEF, a supported correct answer to this question can be the name of a UNICE president only from a certain time period because the QA@CLEF document collection consists of newspaper and newswire articles from 1994 and 1995 (and because there are no documents about the history of UNICE). On the web, there are additional correct answers.[5] Questions with implicit time restriction (30 cases) are excluded from the evaluation so that 170 questions remain for evaluation in InSicht-W3. Alternatives would be to refine these questions by making the temporal restriction explicit or to extend the gold standard by answers that are to be considered correct if working on the web.

Table 1 contains evaluation results for InSicht-W3: the percentages of right, inexact, and wrong answers (separately for non-empty answers and empty answers) and the K1-measure (see (Herrera et al., 2005) for a definition). For comparison, the results of the textual QA system InSicht on the QA@CLEF document collection are shown in the first row. The percentages for non-empty answers differ for right answers and wrong answers. In both aspects, InSicht-W3 is worse than InSicht. The main reason for these changes is that the structure and textual content of documents on the web are much more diverse than in the QA@CLEF collection. For example, InSicht-W3 regarded some sequences of words from unrelated link anchor texts as a sentence, which led to some wrong answers especially for definition questions. Also for empty answers, InSicht-W3 performs worse than InSicht. This is in part due to the too optimistic assumption during answer assessment that all German questions from QA@CLEF 2004 have a correct answer on the web (therefore the column labelled *right empty answers* contains 0.0 for InSicht-W3). However, InSicht-W3 found 12 right answers that InSicht missed. So there is a potential for a fruitful system combination.

The impact of some interesting parameters was evaluated by varying parameter settings (Table 2). The query network quality q_{min} (column 2) is a value between 0 (worst) and 1 (best) that measures how far away a derived query network is from the original semantic network of the question. For example, omitting information from the semantic network for the question (like the first name of a person if also the last name is specified), leads to a reduction of the initial quality value of 1. The value in column 2 indicates at what threshold variant query networks are ignored. Column 3 corresponds to the parameter of word form selection (see Sect. 3.4). The two runs with $d = 300$ and $q_{min} = 0.8$ show that morphological generation pays off, but the effect is smaller than in other document collections. This is probably due to the fact that the large and redundant web often contains answers with the exact word forms from the question. Another interesting aspect found in Table 2 is that even with $d = 500$ results still improve; it remains to be seen at what number of documents performance stays stable (or maybe degrades). The impact of a lower quality threshold q_{min} was not significant. This might change if one operates with a larger parameter d and more inferential rules.

[5] Or just one correct answer, which differs from the one in QA@CLEF, when one interprets the present tense in the question as referring to today.

Table 2: Influence of parameters on InSicht-W3 results. Parameter d is the maximal number of documents used from the search engine results (see Sect. 3.4); q_{min} is the minimal query network quality.

parameter setting			results						
d	q_{min}	morph. generat.	#docs. from first level per quest.	#sent. matching pre. query per quest.	%docs. with matching sent.	right non-empty answ. (%)	inexact answ. (%)	wrong non-empty answ. (%)	K1
100	0.9	frequent	18.1	30.5	59.7	18.8	4.1	1.8	0.13
200	0.9	frequent	34.4	59.0	60.4	20.6	3.5	2.9	0.14
300	0.9	frequent	45.5	76.9	60.2	22.4	3.5	2.4	0.16
300	0.8	frequent	48.4	84.2	61.7	22.4	3.5	2.4	0.16
300	0.8	none	57.3	91.3	61.5	19.4	3.5	3.5	0.12
500	0.8	frequent	68.9	119.8	62.2	22.9	2.9	2.4	0.18

Error analysis and classification is difficult as soon as one steps to the vast web. One could start with a classification of error reasons for wrong empty answers. The error class that can be most easily determined is that the search engine returned no results for the preselection query. 40 of the 170 questions (23.5%) belong to this class. This might surprise users that believe that they can find nearly every bit of information on the web. But there are areas where this assumption is wrong: many QA@CLEF questions relate to very specific events of the year 1994 or 1995. Twelve years ago, the web publishing rate was much lower than today; and even if the relevant pieces of information were on the web at that time (or in the following years), they might have been moved to archives or removed in recent years. Other error reasons are very difficult and labor-intensive to separate:

1. Result pages from the first level do not contain an answer, but if one requests more documents (e.g. by raising the parameter d) result pages with an answer will be found.

2. Result pages from the first level contain an answer, but one or more components of the textual QA system cause that the answer is not found. Subclasses could be defined by adapting the hierarchy that Hartrumpf (2005a) applied to evaluate InSicht.

On average, the 40th search engine result is the first that contains a right answer (in the best InSicht-W3 run).[6] Although this result is for the system and not for a real user (they differ in their strengths and weaknesses in NL understanding), it indicates that human users of web search engines might find the correct answer quite late if at all. This is a strong argument for more advanced, second level tools like a semantic QA system: How many users will read through 40 search engine results and (possibly) 40 underlying web pages?

The answer time of InSicht-W3 currently ranges between 15 and 1200 seconds. The document download time was excluded because it depended on too many external factors (caches, intranet effects, parallel vs. sequential downloads) to be measured consistently and reliably.

5 Related Work

There are few QA systems for German. The system described by Neumann and Xu (2003) works on German web pages. Its general approach differs from InSicht because it relies on shallow, but robust methods, while InSicht builds on sentence parsing and semantic representations. In this respect, InSicht resembles the (English) textual QA system presented by Harabagiu et al. (2001). In contrast to InSicht, this system applies a theorem prover and a large knowledge base to validate candidate answers. An interesting combination of web and textual QA is presented by Vicedo et al. (2005): English and Spanish web documents are used to enhance textual QA in Spanish.

[6]This high number is in part an artifact of the preselection query generation. In a more thorough analysis, human users could be given the NL question and be asked to formulate a corresponding search engine query.

One of the first web QA systems for English was Mulder (Kwok et al., 2001). Mulder parses only the text snippets returned by the search engine, while InSicht-W3 parses the underlying web pages because the text snippets often have omissions ('...') so that full parsing becomes problematic or impossible. InSicht-W3's approach needs more time, especially if the web pages are not in the local cache that InSicht-W3 maintains in order to reduce its bandwidth requirements.

6 Conclusion and Perspectives

In this paper, an existent textual QA system was extended and modified to work successfully on the German web as a virtual document collection. The main results are: precision-oriented extensions and experimentally derived parameter settings are needed to achieve similar performance on the vast web as on small-sized document collections that show higher homogeneity and quality of the contained texts; taking a semantic QA system to the web is feasible as demonstrated in this paper, but answering a question is still expensive in terms of bandwidth and CPU time.

There are several interesting directions for future work. The first level of InSicht-W3 can be improved by finding a better suited search engine or by building and running a new one in a distributed manner. Ideally, it should support arbitrarily complex Boolean queries, parameterized proximity operators like NEAR/N ($N \in \{1,2,\ldots,100\}$), or even linguistically informed operators like *same-sentence* and *same-paragraph*.

The second level (the textual QA system) can be improved by acquiring more inferential knowledge to allow better query expansion. The matching approach can be extended from the unit *sentence* to a larger linguistic unit like paragraph, text, and even text collection. Distributed architectures and algorithms can reduce answer times.

References

Sanda Harabagiu, Dan Moldovan, Marius Paşca, Rada Mihalcea, Mihai Surdeanu, Răzvan Bunescu, Roxana Gîrju, Vasile Rus, and Paul Morărescu. 2001. The role of lexico-semantic feedback in open-domain textual question-answering. In *Proceedings of the 39th Annual Meeting of the Association for Computational Linguistics (ACL-2001)*, pages 274–281, Toulouse, France.

Sven Hartrumpf, Hermann Helbig, and Rainer Osswald. 2003. The semantically based computer lexicon HaGenLex – Structure and technological environment. *Traitement automatique des langues*, 44(2):81–105.

Sven Hartrumpf. 2003. *Hybrid Disambiguation in Natural Language Analysis*. Der Andere Verlag, Osnabrück, Germany.

Sven Hartrumpf. 2005a. Question answering using sentence parsing and semantic network matching. In (Peters et al., 2005), pages 512–521.

Sven Hartrumpf. 2005b. University of Hagen at QA@CLEF 2005: Extending knowledge and deepening linguistic processing for question answering. In Carol Peters, editor, *Results of the CLEF 2005 Cross-Language System Evaluation Campaign, Working Notes for the CLEF 2005 Workshop*. Centromedia, Wien, Austria.

Hermann Helbig. 2006. *Knowledge Representation and the Semantics of Natural Language*. Springer, Berlin.

Jesús Herrera, Anselmo Peñas, and Felisa Verdejo. 2005. Question answering pilot task at CLEF 2004. In (Peters et al., 2005), pages 581–590.

Cody Kwok, Oren Etzioni, and Daniel S. Weld. 2001. Scaling question answering to the web. *ACM Transactions on Information Systems*, 19(3):242–262.

Bernardo Magnini, Alessandro Vallin, Christelle Ayache, Gregor Erbach, Anselmo Peñas, Maarten de Rijke, Paulo Rocha, Kiril Simov, and Richard Sutcliffe. 2005. Overview of the CLEF 2004 multilingual question answering track. In (Peters et al., 2005), pages 371–391.

Günter Neumann and Bogdan Sacaleanu. 2005. Experiments on robust NL question interpretation and multi-layered document annotation for a cross-language question/answering system. In (Peters et al., 2005), pages 411–422.

Günter Neumann and Feiyu Xu. 2003. Mining answers in German web pages. In *Proceedings of the International Conference on Web Intelligence (WI-2003)*, Halifax, Canada.

Carol Peters, Paul Clough, Julio Gonzalo, Gareth J. F. Jones, Michael Kluck, and Bernardo Magnini, editors. 2005. *Multilingual Information Access for Text, Speech and Images: 5th Workshop of the Cross-Language Evaluation Forum, CLEF 2004*, volume 3491 of *LNCS*. Springer, Berlin.

José L. Vicedo, Maximiliano Saiz, Rubén Izquierdo, and Fernando Llopis. 2005. Does English help question answering in Spanish? In (Peters et al., 2005), pages 552–556.

Experiments Adapting an Open-Domain Question Answering System to the Geographical Domain Using Scope-Based Resources

Daniel Ferrés and **Horacio Rodríguez**
TALP Research Center
Software Department
Universitat Politècnica de Catalunya
{dferres, horacio}@lsi.upc.edu

Abstract

This paper describes an approach to adapt an existing multilingual Open-Domain Question Answering (ODQA) system for factoid questions to a Restricted Domain, the Geographical Domain. The adaptation of this ODQA system involved the modification of some components of our system such as: Question Processing, Passage Retrieval and Answer Extraction. The new system uses external resources like GNS Gazetteer for Named Entity (NE) Classification and Wikipedia or Google in order to obtain relevant documents for this domain. The system focuses on a Geographical Scope: given a region, or country, and a language we can semi-automatically obtain multilingual geographical resources (e.g. gazetteers, trigger words, groups of place names, etc.) of this scope. The system has been trained and evaluated for Spanish in the scope of the Spanish Geography. The evaluation reveals that the use of scope-based Geographical resources is a good approach to deal with multilingual Geographical Domain Question Answering.

1 Introduction

Question Answering (QA) is the task of, given a query expressed in Natural Language (NL), retrieving its correct answer (a single item, a text snippet,...). QA has become a popular task in the NL Processing (NLP) research community in the framework of different international ODQA evaluation contests such as: Text Retrieval Conference (TREC) for English, Cross-Lingual Evaluation Forum (CLEF) for European languages, and NTCIR for Asian languages.

In this paper we describe our experiments in the adaptation and evaluation of an ODQA system to a Restricted Domain, the Geographical Domain.

GeoTALP-QA is a multilingual Geographical Domain Question Answering (GDQA) system. This Restricted Domain Question Answering (RDQA) system has been built over an existing ODQA system, TALP-QA, a multilingual ODQA system that processes both factoid and definition questions (see (Ferrés et al., 2005) and (Ferrés et al., 2004)). The system was evaluated for Spanish and English in the context of our participation in the conferences TREC and CLEF in 2005 and has been adapted to a multilingual GDQA system for factoid questions.

As pointed out in (Benamara, 2004), the Geographical Domain (GD) can be considered a middle way between real Restricted Domains and open ones because many open domain texts contain a high density of geographical terms.

Although the basic architecture of TALP-QA has remained unchanged, a set of QA components were redesigned and modified and we had to add some specific components for the GD to our QA system. The basic approach in TALP-QA consists of applying language-dependent processes on both question and passages for getting a language independent semantic representation, and then extracting a set of Semantic Constraints (SC) for each question. Then, an answer extraction algorithm extracts and ranks sentences that satisfy the SCs of the question. Finally, an answer selection module chooses the most appropriate answer.

We outline below the organization of the paper. In the next section we present some characteristics of RDQA systems. In Section 3, we present the overall architecture of GeoTALP-QA and describe briefly its main components, focusing on those components that have been adapted from an ODQA to a GDQA. Then, the Scope-Based Resources needed for the experimentation and the experiments are presented in Sections 4 and 5. In section 6 we present the results obtained over a GD corpus. Finally, in Section 7 and 8 we describe our conclusions and the future work.

2 Restricted Domain QA Systems

RDQAs present some characteristics that prevent us from a direct use of ODQA systems. The most important differences are:

- Usually, for RDQA, the answers are searched in relatively small domain specific collections, so methods based on exploiting the redundancy of answers in several documents are not useful. Furthermore, a highly accurate Passage Retrieval module is required because frequently the answer occurs in a very small set of passages.
- RDQAs are frequently task-based. So, the repertory of question patterns is limited allowing a good accuracy in Question Processing with limited effort.
- User requirements regarding the quality of the answer tend to be higher in RDQA. As (Chung et al., 2004) pointed out, no answer is preferred to a wrong answer.
- In RDQA not only NEs but also domain specific terminology plays a central role. This fact usually implies that domain specific lexicons and gazetteers have to be used.
- In some cases, as in GD, many documents included in the collections are far to be standard NL texts but contain tables, lists, ill-formed sentences, etc. sometimes following a more or less defined structure. Thus, extraction systems based, as our, on the linguistic structure of the sentences have to be relaxed in some way to deal with this kind of texts.

More information about RDQA systems can be found in the ACL 2004 Workshop on QA in Restricted Domains[1] and the AAAI 2005 Worshop on Question Answering in Restricted Domains (Molla and Vicedo, 2005) .

[1] http://acl.ldc.upenn.edu/acl2004/qarestricteddomain/

3 System Description

GeoTALP-QA has been developed within the framework of ALIADO[2] project. The system architecture uses a common schema with three phases that are performed sequentially without feedback: Question Processing (QP), Passage Retrieval (PR) and Answer Extraction (AE). More details about this architecture can be found in (Ferrés et al., 2005) and (Ferrés et al., 2004).

Before describing these subsystems, we introduce some additional knowledge sources that have been added to our system for dealing with the geographic domain and some language-dependent NLP tools for English and Spanish. Our aim is to develop a language independent system (at least able to work with English and Spanish). Language dependent components are only included in the Question Pre-processing and Passage Pre-processing components, and can be easily substituted by components for other languages.

3.1 Additional Knowledge Sources

One of the most important task to deal with the problem of GDQA is to detect and classify NEs with its correct Geographical Subclass (see classes in Section 3.3). We use Geographical scope based Knowledge Bases (KB) to solve this problem. These KBs can be built using these resources:

- **GEOnet Names Server (GNS[3])**. A world-wide gazetteer, excluding the USA and Antarctica, with 5.3 million entries.
- **Geographic Names Information System** (GNIS[4]). A gazetteer with 2.0 million entries about geographic features of the USA.
- **Grammars for creating NE aliases**. Geographic NEs tend to occur in a great variety of forms. It is important to take this into account to avoid losing occurrences. A set of patterns for expanding have been created. (e.g. <toponym>_Mountains, <toponym>_Range, <toponym>_Chain).
- **Trigger Words Lexicon**. A lexicon containing trigger words (including multi-word terms) is used for allowing local disambiguation of ambiguous NE, both in the questions and in the retrieved passages.

[2] **ALIADO**. http://gps-tsc.upc.es/veu/aliado
[3] **GNS**. http://earth-info.nga.mil/gns/html
[4] **GNIS**. http://geonames.usgs.gov/geonames/stategaz

Working with geographical scopes avoids many ambiguity problems, but even in a scope these problems occur:

- **Referent ambiguity problem.** This problem occurs when the same name is used for several locations (of the same or different class). In a question, sometimes it is impossible to solve this ambiguity, and, in this case, we have to accept as correct all of the possible interpretations (or a superclass of them). Otherwise, a trigger phrase pattern can be used to resolve the ambiguity (e.g. "Madrid" is an ambiguous NE, but in the phrase, "comunidad de Madrid" (State of Madrid), ambiguity is solved). Given a scope, we automatically obtain the most common trigger phrase patterns of the scope from the GNS gazetteer.

- **Reference ambiguity problem.** This problem occurs when the same location can have more than one name (in Spanish texts this frequently occurs as many place names occur in languages other than Spanish, as Basque, Catalan or Galician). Our approach to solve this problem is to group together all the geographical names that refer to the same location. All the occurrences of the geographical NEs in both questions and passages are substituted by the identifier of the group they belong to.

  We used the geographical knowledge available in the GNS gazetteer to obtain this geographical NEs groups. First, for each place name in the scope-based GNS gazetteer we obtained all the NEs that have the same feature designation code, latitude and longitude. For each group, we then selected an identifier choosing one of the NE included in it using the following heuristics: the information of the GNS field "native" tells if a place name is native, conventional, a variant, or, is not verified. So we decided the group representative assigning the following order of priorities to the names: native, conventional name, variant name, unverified name. If there is more than one place name in the group with the same name type we decide that the additional length gives more priority to be cluster representative. It is necessary to establish a set of priorities among the different place names of the group because in some retrieval engines (e.g. web search engines) is not possible to do long queries.

3.2 Language-Dependent Processing Tools

A set of general purpose NLP tools are used for Spanish and English. The same tools are used for the linguistic processing of both the questions and the passages (see (Ferrés et al., 2005) and (Ferrés et al., 2004) for a more detailed description of these tools). The tools used for Spanish are:

- *FreeLing*, which performs tokenization, morphological analysis, POS tagging, lemmatization, and partial parsing.
- *ABIONET*, a NE Recognizer and Classifier (NERC) on basic categories.
- *EuroWordNet*, used to obtain a list of synsets, a list of hypernyms of each synset, and the Top Concept Ontology class.

The following tools are used to process English:

- *TnT*, a statistical POS tagger.
- *WordNet lemmatizer 2.0.*
- *ABIONET.*
- *WordNet 1.5.*
- *A modified version of the Collins parser.*
- *Alembic*, a NERC with MUC classes.

3.3 Question Processing

The main goal of this subsystem is to detect the Question Type (QT), the Expected Answer Type (EAT), the question logic predicates, and the question analysis. This information is needed for the other subsystems. We use a language-independent formalism to represent this information.

We apply the processes described above to the the question and passages to obtain the following information:

- Lexical and semantic information for each word: form, lemma, POS tag (Eagles or PTB tag-set), semantic class and subclass of NE, and a list of EWN synsets.
- Syntactic information: syntactic constituent structure of the sentence and the information of dependencies and other relations between these components.

Once this information is obtained we can find the information relevant to the following tasks:

- **Environment Building.** The semantic process starts with the extraction of the semantic relations that hold between the different components identified in the question text. These relations are organized into an ontology of about 100 semantic classes and 25 relations (mostly binary) between them. Both classes and relations are related by taxonomic links. The ontology tries to reflect what is needed for an appropriate representation of the semantic environment of the question (and the expected answer). A set of about 150 rules was built to perform this task. The ontology has been extended for the GD (see below the classes related with this domain).

```
    ENTITY
        ENTITY_PROPER_PLACE
            GEOLOGICAL_REGION
                ARCHIPELAGO
                ISLAND
                LAND_FORM
                    MOUNTAIN
                SEA_FORM
                    CAPE
                    GULF
                    SEA
                WATER_FORM
                    RIVER
            POLITICAL_REGION
                CITY
                CONTINENT
                COUNTY
                COUNTRY
                STATE
ENTITY_QUANTITY
            NUMERIC
MAGNITUDE
            AREA
            LENGTH
            FLOW
            WEIGHT
```

- **Question Classification**. Our ODQA system uses 25 QTs. For the GD we only used 10 Question Types (see Table 1). Only 5 QTs are common with the ODQA QTs, 5 QTs have been specially created for this domain.

Question Type	Expected Answer Type
Count_objects	NUMBER
How_many_people	NUMBER
What_area	MEASURE_AREA
What_flow	MEASURE_FLOW
What_height	MEASURE_HEIGHT
What_length	MEASURE_LENGTH
Where_action	LOCATION_SUBCLASS
Where_location	LOCATION_SUBCLASS
Where_quality	LOCATION_SUBCLASS
Default_class	LOCATION

Table 1: QTs and Expected Answer Types.

In order to determine the QT our system uses a Prolog DCG Parser. This parser uses the following features: word form, word position in the question, lemma and part-of-speech (POS). A set of DCG rules was manually configured in order to ensure a sufficient coverage.

The parser uses external information: geographical NE subclasses, trigger words for each Geographical subclass (e.g. "poblado" (*ville*)), semantically related words of each subclass (e.g. "water" related with *sea* and *river*), and introductory phrases for each Question Type (e.g. "which extension" is a phrase of the QT *What_area*).

- **Semantic Constraints Extraction.** Depending on the QT, a subset of useful items of the environment has to be selected in order to extract the answer. Accordingly, we define the set of relations (the semantic constraints) that are supposed to be found in the answer. These relations are classified as mandatory, (MC), (i.e. they have to be satisfied in the passage) or optional, (OC), (if satisfied the score of the answer is higher). In order to build the semantic constraints for each question, a set of rules has been manually built. A set of 88 rules is used. An example of the constraints extracted from an environment is shown in Table 2. This example shows the question type predicted, the initial predicates extracted from the question, the Environment predicates, the MCs and the OCs. MCs are *entity(4)* and *i_en_city(6)*. The first predicate refers to token number 4 ("autonomia" (*state*)) and the last predicate refers to token number 6 ("Barcelona").

Question	¿ A qué autonomía pertenece Barcelona? (At which state pertains Barcelona?)
Q. Type	*where_location*
Predicates	*city('Barcelona'),state(X), pertains('Barcelona',X)*
Environment	*action(5), participant_in_event(5,4), theme_of_event(5,6),prep(4,2),entity(4), i_en_proper_place(6),det(4,3),qu(3)*
Mandatory Constraints	*entity(4),i_en_city(6)*
Optional Constraints	*action(5),theme_of_event(5,6), participant_in_event(5,4),prep(4,2), type_of_location(5,5,i_en_state), property(5,5,pertenecer,3,6)*

Table 2: Question Analysis example.

3.4 Passage Retrieval

We use two different approaches for Passage Retrieval. The first one uses a pre-processed corpus as a document collection. The second one uses the web as document collection.

3.4.1 Off-line Corpus Retrieval

This approach uses a pre-processed and indexed corpus with Scope-related Geographical Information as a document collection for Passage Retrieval. The processed information was used for indexing the documents. Storing this information allows us to avoid the pre-processing step after retrieval. The Passage Retrieval algorithm used is the same of our ODQA system: a data-driven query relaxation technique with dynamic passages implemented using Lucene IR engine API (See (Ferrés et al., 2005) for more details).

3.4.2 Online Web Snippet Retrieval

The other approach uses a search-engine to get snippets with relevant information. We expect to get a high recall with few snippets. In our experiments, we chose Google as the search-engine using a boolean retrieval schema that takes advantage of its phrase search option and the Geographical KB to create queries that can retrieve highly relevant snippets. We try to maximize the number of relevant sentences with only one query per question.

The algorithm used to build the queries is simple. First, some expansion methods described below can be applied over the keywords. Then, stop-words (including normal stop-words and some trigger words) are removed. Finally, only the Nouns and Verbs are extracted from the keywords list. The expansion methods used are:

- **Trigger Words Joining (TWJ).** Uses the trigger words list and the trigger phrase pattern list (automatically generated from GNS) to join trigger phrases (e.g. "isla Conejera" o "Sierra de los Pirineos").

- **Trigger Words Expansion (TWE).** This expansion is applied to the NEs that were not detected as a trigger phrase. The expansion uses its location subclass to create a keyword with the pattern: *TRIGGER* + *NE* (e.g. "Conejera" is expanded to: ("isla Conejera" OR "Conejera")).

- **GNS Grouping Expansion (CE).** Noun Phrase expansion based on the groups generated from GNS Gazetteer.

- **Question-based Expansion (QBE).** This method appends keywords or expands the query depending on the question type. As an example, in the case of a question classified as *What_length*, trigger words and units associated to the question class like *"longitud"* (*length*) and *"kilómetros"* (*kilometers*) are appended to the query.

3.5 Answer Extraction

We used two systems for Answer Extraction: our ODQA system (adapted for the GD) and a frequency based system.

3.5.1 ODQA Extraction

The linguistic process of analyzing passages is similar to the process carried out on questions and leads to the construction of the environment of each sentence. Then, a set of extraction rules are applied following an iterative approach. In the first iteration all the MC have to be satisfied by at least one of the candidate sentences. Then, the iteration proceeds until a threshold is reached by relaxing the MC. The relaxation process of the set of semantic constraints is performed by means of structural or semantic relaxation rules, using the semantic ontology. The extraction process consists on the application of a set of extraction rules on the set of sentences that have satisfied the MC. The Knowledge Source used for this process is a set of extraction rules owning a credibility score. Each QT has its own subset of extraction rules that leads to the selection of the answer.

In order to select the answer from the set of candidates, the following scores are computed and accumulated for each candidate sentence: i) the rule score (which uses factors such as the confidence of the rule used, the relevance of the OC satisfied in the matching, and the similarity between NEs occurring in the candidate sentence and the question), ii) the passage score, iii) a semantic score (see (Ferrés et al., 2005)) , iv) the extraction rule relaxation level score. The answer to the question is the candidate with the best global score.

3.5.2 Frequency-Based Extraction

This extraction algorithm is quite simple. First, all snippets are pre-processed. Then, we make a ranked list of all the tokens satisfying the expected answer type of the question. The score of each token in the snippets is computed using the following formula:

$$Score(tk_i) = \sum_{o \in Occurrence(tk_i)} \frac{1}{snippet\_rank(o)}$$

Finally, the top-ranked token is extracted.

4 Resources for Scope-Based Experiments

In this section we describe how we obtained the resources needed to do experiments in the Spanish Geography domain using Spanish. These resources were: the question corpus (validation and test), the document collection required by the offline ODQA Passage Retrieval, and the geographical scope-based resources. Finally, we describe the experiments performed.

4.1 Language and Scope based Geographical Question Corpus

We obtained a corpus of Geographical questions from Albayzin, a speech corpus (Diaz et al., 1998) that contains a geographical subcorpus with utterances of questions about the geography of Spain in Spanish. We obtained from Albayzin a set of 6887 question patterns. We analyzed this corpus and we extracted the following type of questions: Partial Direct, Partial Indirect, and Imperative Interrogative factoid questions with a simple level of difficulty (e.g. questions without nested questions). We selected a set of 2287 question patterns. As a question corpus we randomly selected a set of 177 question patterns from the previous selection (see Table 3). These patterns have been randomly instantiated with Geographical NEs of the Albayzin corpus. Then, we searched the answers in the Web and the Spanish Wikipedia (SW). The results of this process were: 123 questions with answer in the SW and the Web, 33 questions without answer in the SW but with answer using the Web, and finally, 21 questions without answer (due to the fact that some questions when instantiated cannot be answered (e.g. which sea bathes the coast of Madrid?)). We divided the 123 questions with answer in the SW in two sets: 61 questions for development (setting thresholds and other parameters) and 62 for test.

¿A qué comunidad autónoma pertenece el <PICO>?
At which state pertains <PEAK>?
¿Cuál es el capital de <COMUNIDAD>?
Which is the capital of <STATE>?
¿Cuál es la comunidad en la que desemboca el <RÍO>?
What is the state in which <RIVER> flows into?
¿Cuál es la extensión de <COMUNIDAD>?
Which is the extension of <STATE>?
Longitud del río <RÍO>.
Length of river <RIVER>.
¿Cuántos habitantes tiene la <COMUNIDAD>?
How many people does <STATE> has?

Table 3: Some question patterns from Albayzin.

4.2 Document Collection for ODQA Passage Retrieval

In order to test our ODQA Passage Retrieval system we need a document collection with sufficient geographical information to resolve the questions of Albayzin corpus. We used the filtered Spanish Wikipedia[5]. First, we obtained the original set of documents (26235 files). Then, we selected two sets of 120 documents about the Spanish geography domain and the non-Spanish geography domain. Using these sets we obtained a set of Topic Signatures (TS) (Lin and Hovy, 2000) for the Spanish geography domain and another set of TS for the non-Spanish geography domain. Then, we used these TS to filter the documents from Wikipedia, and we obtained a set of 8851 documents pertaining to the Spanish geography domain. These documents were pre-processed and indexed.

4.3 Geographical Scope-Based Resources

A Knowledge Base (KB) of Spanish Geography has been built using four resources:

- GNS: We obtained a set of 32222 non-ambiguous place names of Spain.
- Albayzin Gazetteer: a set of 758 places.
- A Grammar for creating NE aliases. We created patterns for the summit and state classes (the ones with more variety of forms), and we expanded this patterns using the entries of Albayzin.
- A lexicon of 462 trigger words.

We obtained a set of 7632 groups of place names using the grouping process over GNS. These groups contain a total of 17617 place

[5]**Spanish Wikipedia**. http://es.wikipedia.org

names, with an average of 2.51 place names per group. See in Figure 1 an example of a group where the canonical term appears underlined.

{*Cordillera Pirenaica*, *Pireneus*, *Pirineos*, *Pyrenaei Montes*, *Pyrénées*, *Pyrene*, *Pyrenees*}

Figure 1: Example of a group obtained from GNS.

In addition, a set of the most common trigger phrases in the domain has been obtained from the GNS gazetteer (see Table 4).

	Geographical Scope	
	Spain	UK
Top-ranked Trigger Phrases	*TRIGGER* de *NE*	*NE TRIGGER*
	TRIGGER NE	*TRIGGER NE*
	TRIGGER del *NE*	*TRIGGER* of *NE*
	TRIGGER de la *NE*	*TRIGGER* a' *NE*
	TRIGGER de las *NE*	*TRIGGER* na *NE*

Table 4: Sample of the top-ranked trigger phrases automatically obtained from GNS gazetteer for the geography of Spain and UK.

5 Experiments

We have designed some experiments in order to evaluate the accuracy of the GDQA system and its subsystems (QP, PR, and AE). For PR, we evaluated the web-based snippet retrieval using Google with some variants of expansions, versus our ODQA Passage Retrieval with the corpus of the SW. Then, the passages (or snippets) retrieved by the best PR approach were used by the two different Answer Extraction algorithms. The ODQA Answer Extractor has been evaluated taking into account the answers that have a supported context in the set of passages (or snippets). Finally, we evaluated the global results of the complete QA process with the different Answer Extractors: ODQA and Frequency-Based.

6 Results

This section evaluates the behavior of our GDQA system over a test corpus of 62 questions and reports the errors detected on the best run. We evaluated the three main components of our system and the global results.

- **Question Processing**. The Question Classification task has been manually evaluated. This subsystem has an accuracy of 96.77%.

- **Passage Retrieval**. The evaluation of this subsystem was performed using a set of correct answers (see Table 5). We computed the *answer accuracy*: it takes into account the number of questions that have a correct answer in its set of passages.

Retrieval Mode	Accuracy at N passages/snippets			
	N=10	N=20	N=50	N=100
Google	0.6612	0.6935	0.7903	0.8225
+TWJ	0.6612	0.6774	0.7419	0.7580
+TWJ+TWE	0.6612	0.6774	0.7419	0.7580
+CE	0.6612	0.6774	0.7741	0.8064
+QBE	0.8064	0.8387	0.9032	0.9354
+TWJ+QB+CE	0.7903	0.8064	0.8548	0.8870
Google+All	0.7903	0.8064	0.8548	0.8870
ODQA+Wiki	0.4354	0.4516	0.4677	0.5000

Table 5: Passage Retrieval results (refer to section 3.4.2 for detailed information of the different query expansion acronyms).

- **Answer Extraction**. The evaluation of the ODQA Answer Extractor subsystem is shown in Table 6. We evaluated the accuracy taking into account the number of correct and supported answers by the passages divided by the total number of questions that have a supported answer in its set of passages. This evaluation has been done using the results of the top-ranked retrieval configuration over the development set: the *Google+TWJ+QB+CE* configuration of the snippet retriever.

Accuracy at N Snippets		
N=10	N=20	N=50
0.2439 (10/41)	0.3255 (14/43)	0.3333 (16/48)

Table 6: Results of the ODQA Answer Extraction subsystem (accuracy).

In Table 7 are shown the global results of the two QA Answer Extractors used (ODQA and Frequency-Based). The passages retrieved by the *Google+TWJ+QB+CE* configuration of the snippet retriever were used.

	Accuracy	
Num. Snippets	ODQA	Freq-based
10	0.1774 (11/62)	0.5645 (35/62)
20	0.2580 (16/62)	0.5967 (37/62)
50	0.3387 (21/62)	0.6290 (39/62)

Table 7: QA results over the test set.

We analyzed the 23 questions that fail in our best run. The analysis detected that 10 questions had no answer in its set of passages. In 5 of these questions it is due to have a non common question or location. The other 5 questions have problems with ambiguous trigger words (e.g. *capital*) that confuse the web-search engine. On the other hand, 13 questions had the answer in its set of passages, but were incorrectly answered. The reasons are mainly due to the lack of passages with the answer (8), answer validation and spatial-reasoning (3), multilabel Geographical NERC (1), and more context in the snippets (1).

7 Evaluation and Conclusions

This paper summarizes our experiments adapting an ODQA to the GD and its evaluation in Spanish in the scope of the Spanish Geography. Out of 62 questions, our system provided the correct answer to 39 questions in the experiment with the best results.

Our Passage Retrieval for ODQA offers less attractive results when using the SW corpus. The problem of using SW to extract the answers is that it gives few documents with the correct answer, and, it is difficult to extract the answer because the documents contain tables, lists, ill-formed sentences, etc. Our ODQA AE needs a grammatically well-structured text to extract correctly the answers. The QA system offers a low performance (33% of accuracy) when using this AE over the web-based retrieved passages. In some cases, the snippets are cut and we could expect a better performance retrieving the whole documents from Google.

On the other hand, web-based snippet retrieval, with only one query per question, gives good results in Passage Retrieval. The QA system with the Frequency-Based AE obtained better results than with the ODQA AE (62.9% of accuracy).

Finally, we conclude that our approach with Geographical scope-based resources are notably helpful to deal with multilingual Geographical Domain Question Answering.

8 Future Work

As a future work we plan to improve the AE module using a semantic analysis with extended contexts (i.e. more than one sentence) and adding some spatial reasoning. We also want to improve the retrieval by crawling relevant documents from web search-engines instead of using snippets. This could be a good method to find more sentences with supported answers. Finally, we expect to do tests with English in another scope.

Acknowledgements

This work has been partially supported by the European Commission (CHIL, IST-2004-506909) and the Spanish Research Dept. (ALIADO, TIC2002-04447-C02). Daniel Ferrés is supported by a UPC-Recerca grant from Universitat Politècnica de Catalunya (UPC). TALP Research Center is recognized as a Quality Research Group (2001 SGR 00254) by DURSI, the Research Department of the Catalan Government.

References

F. Benamara. 2004. Cooperative Question Answering in Restricted Domains: the WEBCOOP Experiment. In *Proceedings of the Workshop Question Answering in Restricted Domains, within ACL-2004.*

H. Chung, Y. Song, K. Han, D. Yoon, J. Lee, H. Rim, and S. Kim. 2004. A Practical QA System in Restricted Domains. In *Proceedings of the Workshop Question Answering in Restricted Domains, within ACL-2004.*

J. Diaz, A. Rubio, A. Peinado, E. Segarra, N. Prieto, and F. Casacuberta. 1998. Development of Task-Oriented Spanish Speech Corpora. In *Procceedings of the First International Conference on Language Resources and Evaluation*, pages 497–501, Granada, Spain, May. ELDA.

D. Ferrés, S. Kanaan, A. Ageno, E. González, H. Rodríguez, M. Surdeanu, and J. Turmo. 2004. The TALP-QA System for Spanish at CLEF 2004: Structural and Hierarchical Relaxing of Semantic Constraints. In C. Peters, P. Clough, J. Gonzalo, G. J. F. Jones, M. Kluck, and B. Magnini, editors, *CLEF*, volume 3491 of *Lecture Notes in Computer Science*, pages 557–568. Springer.

D. Ferrés, S. Kanaan, E. González, A. Ageno, H. Rodríguez, M. Surdeanu, and J. Turmo. 2005. TALP-QA System at TREC 2004: Structural and Hierarchical Relaxation Over Semantic Constraints. In *Proceedings of the Text Retrieval Conference (TREC-2004).*

C-Y. Lin and E. Hovy. 2000. The automated acquisition of topic signatures for text summarization. In *COLING*, pages 495–501. Morgan Kaufmann.

D. Molla and J.L. Vicedo. 2005. *AAAI-05 Workshop on Question Answering in Restricted Domains*. AAAI Press. to appear.

Association for Computational Linguistics
209 N. Eighth Street
Stroudsburg, Pennsylvania 18360